JESUS Ph.D.

PSYCHOLOGIST

JESUS *Ph.D.* PSYCHOLOGIST

TOM BRUNO

Bridge-Logos *Publishers*

Gainesville, Florida 32614 USA

Jesus Ph.D. Psychologist

by Thomas Bruno
Copyright © 2000 by Bridge-Logos Publishers
Library of Congress Catalog Card Number: 00-105082
International Standard Book Number: 0-88270-824-4

Published by:
Bridge-Logos *Publishers*
PO Box 141630
Gainesville, FL 32614
http://www.bridgelogos.com

Dedication

Dedicated to the loving memory of my late son Scott, whose light among us went out far too soon!

Dedicated to all who are involved in the process of healing and helping others understand the truth of our existence.

Dedicated to my grandchildren, David, Melissa, Justin, Michael, Kathryn with whom the hope for the future lies.

Acknowledgments

My sincere thanks to my Publisher Guy Morrell and his staff who have been enthusiastic about my vision for this book. To Michele, my wife who supported me in my long hours and endless obsession with the manuscript.

I am blessed to have four delightful children, which includes Scott who passed away three years ago. Christina, Tom and Matthew have always been excited about my writings.

My thanks to the office staff, Laura Mahler and Joyce Peitz who always had time to listen to my "latest and greatest idea."

A special thanks to Dr. Tony Morici who never wavered in his support of me and this endeavor.

Then there is Diana Chernoff who liked the book even in its roughest form and always teased me with what the future might hold.

Vange Puszcz was helpful with the first contact of this book and started the long process of proof reading. It was Cindy Crosby that I was fortunate to have as editor who brought it to its final form. My thanks to Paul Alley who has been a good friend and support person.

Finally, my appreciation to Jim Russell and Mike Fonfara both fellow ministers in the faith who have been supportive and helpful in every way to make this book a reality.

This book was a group effort and to all who helped my sincere thanks!

Tom

July 11, 2000

Contents

The Power of Relationships

Preface

Jesus is the Great Psychologist. Who could know us better than the Author of life?

Jesus, Ph.D., Psychologist, is a down-to-earth guide to help us understand the truths Jesus shared that shape and change lives. All of His principles have psychological implications, specifically three:

- · Self-mastery
- · Action
- · Relationships

Self-mastery is the inward journey. Relationships are about our interaction with others and our contemporary society. Action is the bridge that connects our inward and outward journeys.

To read about these principles is not enough. Our goal must be know them and to live by them; to take them into our hearts and gain wisdom to live life to the fullest!

This is the supreme gift: Experiencing life as the Great Psychologist would have us experience it.

Introduction

Life isn't fair!

I used to blame God for this. Then, there was a time when I was audacious enough to believe I should forgive Him for it. Slowly, I realized that God does not police our world, and we play a part in its dysfunction. Finally, I arrived at the belief that the mess in the world is our own fault.

Jesus stepped into our "unfair" world. He saw the injustices and unfairness firsthand. Despite His own fair and unblemished behavior, Jesus was treated unfairly. From the time of His birth, when King Herod sought to kill Him, to His death at the hands of the Roman Centurions, Jesus endured the unfairness of life. He offered those around Him—and us today—spiritual truths by which we can live and enter into the full dimension of what God has planned for us since the beginning of time.

This book is about the Great Psychologist. It is a book about light and darkness, love and death, and truth and righteousness vs. lies and deception. It's about freedom and liberation from addictions that hold us in bondage and sap the life from legions of individuals. It's about faith that moves mountains in the midst of despair and hopelessness. It's about lost opportunities and new possibilities. It's about barriers, and bridges.

Our world has taken a wrong turn on the freeway and is hurtling toward a dead-end. We are reaping tragic results in our society as a consequence of our behavior. Yet, if we take the high road, which few choose to tread, we can begin to understand this brief moment called life. This is a book for those seeking to understand life. It is not only a prelude to eternity, but also a preparation for it.

Come meet the Great Psychologist of heaven and earth, who through His work and ministry tries to level the playing field and make life a little fairer. You have an appointment with Him—He's waiting to listen, to care, and to say "I love you. I will always be with you."

If you take His psychological insights to heart, your life can change, beginning right now! It takes more than just hearing His words. Jesus wants you to understand His words, and tuck the knowledge of them deep into your mind and heart. He wants you to make His truths your own. Then your deeds will spring from your inner well of belief.

His door is open now. Come and meet Him.

Jesus, The Great Psychologist

He had no formal office with set hours. He didn't hang out a public shingle displaying His credentials, and His name wasn't listed in the Yellow Pages of the telephone directory. No glossy business cards. No framed diploma on the wall. He never billed Blue Cross for His services, or used personality tests and diagnostic devices on His patients.

Jesus' office was the open road, framed by sky and earth and trees. His confessional booth was portable and always open. He counseled men and women, the rich and the poor, the helpless and the hopeless, and the powerful and weak.

Attempts to classify Him as a Freudian, Behaviorist, Jungian or a Humanist would be a distraction. Instead, He took truth where He saw it, and used it where it was needed.

Traditionally, psychology is said to be the study of human behavior. If Jesus' behavior was evaluated by a psychologist in a contemporary psychological arena, He might not fare too well. Imagine, if you will, Jesus walking into a typical 21st century clinic.

First of all, Jesus claimed He heard voices. At times, you might observe Him looking up into the clouds and talking. He believed people were out to get Him. He had delusions of grandeur—indeed, He thought He was the Son of God! He stated confidently that He was not of this world, and that His stay here was brief. He also said that He would be going back to the world He came from.

He walked on water. He healed people. He claimed that He could bring people back from the dead, and that He even talked to prophets from the Old Testament who had been dead for hundreds of years! He constantly talked about the horrible death He was going to die, and insisted He would come back to life after three days.

A modern psychologist would commit Jesus to a mental hospital for a long, long, time. Diagnosis: Paranoid schizophrenia with delusions of grandeur and/or persecution. Most psychologists would not have taken His case—unless He had good insurance. The prognosis would be dim. And after a session with such a client, the psychologist might have a need to make his own psychological appointment!

Yet, Jesus did hear voices. He did talk to His Father, who was invisible, and He was pursued by those who desired his death. He was the Great Psychologist!

A psychologist is someone who studies human behavior and applies this knowledge to the healing and well-being of an individual. The psychologist focuses on the healing process, helping the individual with insights that implement the growth process.

People frequently ask me what I do for a living. I often get tired of the question, and the stereotypes it conjures up in people's minds when I say I am a psychologist. So, I often reply that I am in public relations, or human resources, and hope the person asking me will not probe more deeply.

When I was a minister, and people at a dinner party would find out, the swearing and dirty jokes would cease. Now, when I'm in a social situation and say I'm a psychologist, people stop talking altogether because they are intimidated.

In frustration one day, when a successful lawyer asked me what I did for a living, I told him I was a squire.

"What in the world is a squire?" he asked, puzzled.

"Well," I said, "Did you ever read about King Arthur and the Knights of the Round Table?"

"Yeah, I have," he said.

"Well, I'm a squire to the Knight in Shining Armor."

He laughed as if I had lost my marbles.

"Let me tell you what a squire does," I said. "In the age of King Arthur, the squire helped the knight get ready for battle. He picked out the right armor, helped the knight get dressed, and then pointed the way to the dragon or the enemy. He showed the knight the enemy's vulnerable spots. When the knight entered the battlefield, the squire became a one-man cheering section."

"That's what you do? Don't quit your day job," he snapped. Then smiling politely, he excused himself and spent the rest of the evening as far away from me and my perceived dragons as he could.

As a psychologist, I am a squire to my clients. I feel it is an honor to be asked to accompany another person as he goes out to conquer the giants in his life. The invitation to walk alongside a wounded person on their journey of life is a sacred task. And, while I cannot fight their battles, I have learned that giving others the tools to fight is very empowering. I listen rather than spout advice, encourage rather than push too hard; and love rather than judge. I seek to understand their difficulties, and be a cheerleader in their recovery.

Jesus promised to share with us the tools we need to do battle, and most important, to come alongside of us no matter what. In a small way, Jesus is also a squire for us—and much more, as well!

Let's take a look at Jesus, the Psychologist. At The Center for Humanistic Studies, we use the terminology "epobe" to describe a clearing of the mind, as if you are starting with a blank piece of paper with no writing on it. I invite you to put aside any prejudices or preconceived ideas you have so your mind will be receptive to "new truth." This is how I began my own journey investigating Jesus as the Great Psychologist.

Being a psychologist requires establishing solid ingredients in a client-patient relationship. Using the guidelines of Carl Rogers, a famous psychologist who has been a tremendous influence on me, I offer these six conditions as existing with every person that came into contact with Jesus the Psychologist.

1. They had a relationship with Jesus. For some it was minimal, for others, it was a deep relationship. Before change can occur, there must be contact, or a relationship that is established.

2. They had a need. The people Jesus helped were vulnerable and anxious. They had an awareness that something was missing in their lives. They were often broken, and motivated by pain.

3. The Psychologist was whole. Jesus, Ph.D., was able through His wholeness to assist those who came to Him for help.

4. The Psychologist offered unconditional love. Jesus' acceptance of people was not based on conditions. He accepted those He helped without being judgmental.

5. He empathized. Jesus understood His "patients'" feelings. He felt their pain, and desired to intervene and help them become whole again. Think of Jesus, weeping alongside Mary and Martha when they lost their brother, Lazarus!

6. His patients accepted His help. They were willing to let Him help them initiate change in their lives. There was faith on the part of the "client."

Change and transformation occurred over and over again in the encounters between "clients" and the Great Psychologist. So dynamic were these changes that resulted from these personal encounters that we can not help but stand in awe of His power!

Jesus, the Psychologist, taught in two very different, yet related, ways.

He taught by example, or modeling. For thirty-three years He walked among us in ancient Palestine. His early years are obscure, but His later years of ministry are well-documented by the writers of the Gospels: Matthew, Mark, Luke, and John. Unlike a modern psychologist, whose personal life may be a mystery to her clients, we know that what Jesus taught was in harmony with how He lived. He forgave others, while teaching that we must forgive "seventy times seven." He taught about peace, and was at peace with Himself. His acts of compassion and healing stand so boldly that no words are necessary to communicate this truth.

He gave us His spoken Word. Other words will pass away; His words will never pass away.

Perhaps you think I shouldn't be mixing "religion" and "psychology." Throughout this book, I use the words "spirituality" and "religion." When I use the word "religion," I am talking about the traditional Christian faith taught by the Church. When I use the word "spirituality," which I prefer, I am referring to your own personal beliefs about God, His kingdom, and the universe in which we live.

Jesus would be surprised by our current dichotomy between what is "spiritual" and what is "psychological." It is this division that has gotten us into our present state of ill affairs! It is this division, which often favors psychology over spirituality, that creates such a vacuum in our society. It is a false model, which tells us we can have psychological well-being without grounding and rooting it in spirituality. No wonder we are surrounded by such sickness in our society! When we neglect our spiritual side, we reap the consequences. Ernie Larson, a leader in the field of treating addictions, said he believes our addictions are really a search for God.

What consequences do we reap when we neglect our spiritual side? A few of the consequences that I hear about from my clients include: substance addiction, sexual addiction, domestic abuse, a feeling of meaningless, incest, loss of morals, general depression, difficulty with intimacy, a lack of self-esteem.

Modern society is naïve to think it can address these deep-rooted problems that plague us without a spiritual base. It was Jung who said that every psychological problem is ultimately a matter of religion. Our spiritual health is absolutely necessary for us to have psychological health.

At the same time we care for ourselves spiritually, we need to not neglect our psychological health. Spirituality is not a substitute for what we need to do psychologically in our lives. We need to build a bridge between spirituality and psychology, and weave both into the fabric of our lives.

Jesus did not identify or divide His truths into different categories. Imagine your life as a brightly painted chariot, pulled by two equally strong, beautiful white horses. Their names are "psyche" and "spirit." Together, running side-by-side, they pull your chariot of life. When one is out of stride, it affects the other, and your chariot falters. Neither horse is meant to outrun or overpower the other. Balance is the key.

I believe we need to establish a new model that has room for both psychology and spirituality. We need a holistic model that addresses the needs of a whole person. Jesus gives us this model.

Look at Jesus, the psychologist, with new eyes and a new heart! He offers wisdom and insights for the spiritual journey.

Why Jesus is the Great Psychologist

He is a good listener.
He loves people.
He is intuitive.
He focuses on solutions.
He believes in our ability to change our lives.
He is compassionate.
He loves us unconditionally.
He teaches us to focus.
He was fully human, and had feelings and thoughts like we do.
He teaches us to ask for what we need.
He urges us to work through our fears.
He helps us to transcend our negativism.
He tells us to release our anger.
He stresses accountability.
He is well-grounded.
He is psychologically healthy.
His actions and words are motivated by love.
He shows us the need for purpose in our lives.

He has a deep understanding of suffering.

[1]To us a son is given; and the government will be upon His shoulder, and His name will be called Wonderful Counselor.

(Isaiah 9:6, NKJV)

Between us and Heaven or Hell
there is only life
which is the frailest thing
in the world
—Blaise Pascal, Pensees (1670)

THE POWER OF

SELF-MASTERY

He Taught Us to Take the Inward Journey

"There is a great deal of unmapped country within us."
—George Eliot

In the movie, *Chariots of Fire,* we meet Eric Liddell, a Scottish Christian who decides to postpone a missionary career in China to run in the 1924 Olympic Games. He and his fellow runners are described as having "hope in their hearts, and wings on their feet."

Throughout the movie, Liddell is challenged with balancing the importance of his running with the importance of his faith. His sister, Jeanie sees his running as a distraction and encourages Eric to return to his missionary work. Knowing that his running is part of God's plan for his life, he tells his sister "God has made me for a purpose, and I am fast!"

In one moving scene, a supportive group of well-wishers gathers around him in the rain, eager to hear his thoughts about life and running. Liddell says he has no set formula for winning the race, and compares the race to his personal faith. He then states, "and where does that power come from to see the race to its end, it comes from within. Jesus said, 'Behold, the Kingdom of God is within you.'"[1]

Later in the movie, Liddell refuses to run when his event is scheduled on the Sabbath—a decision that makes national headlines! Then, he is allowed to run in the 400-meter event. In a stunning scene, he gloriously crosses the finish line first, winning a gold medal for Scotland. He is a national hero. Eric listened to the voice within him and obeyed it.

Jesus encourages us to take the inward journey, the journey of the heart. In some ways, it is the shortest journey you will ever take. In other ways, it is the longest. It is a never-ending journey that will evolve and continue throughout our lifetime.

There are two journeys in life: the inward journey and the outward journey. Unfortunately, many people take the outward journey first. The outward journey is forced on us by life, which we must take, ready or not. The inward journey is entirely voluntary. Some will choose to never take it.

Those who do not take the inward journey are obvious. They are shallow, skin-deep. There is no depth to them. We engage them in conversation, but we walk away bored.

Perhaps these are the people T.S. Elliott writes about in his poem, *The Hollow Men,* published in 1925:

We are the hollow men

We are the stuffed men

Leaning together

Headpiece filled with straw. Alas

Our dried voices, when

We whisper together

Are quiet and meaningless

As wind in dry grass

Or rats feet over broken glass

In our dry cellar

Shape without form,

Shade without colour,

Paralysed force, gesture without motion.[2]

The hollow men are still with us, more numerous than ever.

To take the inward journey, we must engage with ourselves, and engage with God. We benefit from moving consciously toward self-knowledge. Or, as the ancients urged, "know thyself." Socrates said "The unexamined life is not worth living." From the earliest writings of the philosophers and mystics, we are urged to take the inward journey.

Gary made an appointment with me to try and find some answers for his life. At his first visit, he declared "I am forty-three years old, and I don't know who I am or why I do what I do!" He had experienced much suffering and pain, and had made many mistakes. He remembered things he had said that he wished he could take back, and things he had done that he wanted to undo.

The answers to what Gary is seeking can only come from the journey within. Much of his agony was caused by not taking his inner path more seriously. We always pay a price when we don't choose the inward journey, and those around us may suffer as well. Gary is late in starting his inward journey, but there is still light on the road for him to travel by.

As you take your inner journey, you may discover that there are thoughts you have kept to yourself. There may be secrets you have kept hidden; secrets you have never shared. These thoughts may be unconscious. Too few of us have met our real selves, and fewer of us yet like ourselves when we meet ourselves! Yet, we are the only creatures in all of creation that have this sense of knowing, and the ability to contemplate life and death. The Psalmist, searching on his own inward journey, wrote [3]"Why are you cast down, O my soul, and why are you disquieted within me?"

Two years ago as I continued my own inward journey, an enlightened friend of mine helped me understand how a traumatic incident that I experienced at the age of nine impacted other events in my life. This insightful discovery gave me much-needed closure, and also taught me that the inward journey is never completed—it is always evolving, regardless of our age. Here is one truth: "We are never too old to learn something new, and the only time we are permitted to stop learning is when we breath that last breathe of air." I am constantly reminded that "I want to be alive when I die."

I often ask individuals who are seeking internal knowledge about themselves this question: "What is your existential apriori?" They usually give me a puzzled look, and ask me to explain. I rephrase the question in simpler terms: "What is the principle by which you live and interpret life?" Surprisingly, many people don't know! They must think about it for a while before they are able to respond.

Whether we can articulate it or not, we are all operating on principles we have accepted as personal truth. These principles are the thoughts and feelings we act upon, consciously or unconsciously.

When we begin the inward journey, one of our first tasks is to discover these principles. Think of it as figuring out what "furniture" you have inside of you and how it is arranged. Find out what you think. Get in touch with your feelings and emotions. By finding out who you are now, it will help you know who you want to be.

How important is this inward journey? It is crucial—our psychological well-being is at stake. Because our society has created a sharp division between "feeling" and "thinking," we have individuals going through life choosing to do one or the other—and not integrating both! Women are often stereotyped as "feelings" and men as "thinking." It is true, that when I ask my male clients what they feel, they have a more difficult time knowing and getting in touch with their feelings than my female clients. Women seem to be more naturally in touch with their feelings, and more easily express them. Part of this is cultural training.

Yet, it is not a question of "feeling" or "thinking," it is a matter of doing both! Life calls for us to truly feel and truly think, and put both of these processes in harmony with each other.

Three dividends can come out of the inward journey, related to our own self-examination:

First, there is change. I can change and modify what I want to work on in my life. With this self-knowledge I can move toward an understanding of my own personal uniqueness. You cannot be authentic in significant relationships, if you don't know who you are! This self-knowledge leads to peace of mind and internal harmony.

Next, there is self-love. Surprisingly, sadly, many have not given themselves this liberating, rewarding gift.

Consequently, we are our own worst enemy! We need no critics; we criticize ourselves. When Jesus summarized the Law of the Old Testament, He said we should love our neighbor as ourselves. Jesus assumed we do love ourselves! There is as much of a command here from Jesus to love ourselves as to love our neighbors. When people are motivated by a tragic, painful self-hate, they perpetuate hate crimes and go on shooting sprees on playgrounds and in schools, they may actually be loving their neighbor as they love themselves.

Then, there is self-esteem. This is an outgrowth of self-love, and a gift only you can give to yourself. Oh, the pain and agony of suffering from low self-esteem! It is an albatross tied around our necks, it is the thief that steals our happiness. It is best labeled the silent epidemic, for while many try to camouflage the low thoughts they have of themselves behind forced smiles, they spend long hours in anguish alone in the quiet, dark closets of their hearts. I lived in this dark valley for many years, and know how difficult it is to find healthy self-esteem. When you can be happy without sabotaging yourself, you have achieved healthy self-esteem.

The higher our self-esteem, the greater number of choices we have. The lower our self-esteem, the narrower our world appears to be. When we have low self-esteem we push others away from us—at the moment we so desperately need and want their love! When our self-esteem is high, we radiate its energy of warmth and goodness and others are drawn to us like magnets. They ask us what the source of our energy is.

It is not until we love and see our own unique worth that our life will take a giant positive leap forward. Until then, we will remain in the pits.

Jesus taught us that every life is significant no matter how insignificant others may view that life. Honor your life, and fight for every possibility that is yours!

Christopher knew this dark despair of low self-esteem. After being convicted of theft, he was sentenced to a year in prison. Chris was only in his thirties, and had a faithful woman who believed and stood by him. Chris believed in God, and realized he had made a mess of his life with his poor decisions. He was plagued by self-doubt and a deep sense of inferiority, and in one sense, believed he was getting what he deserved in life. Chris did not love himself.

This all changed when he began going to the prison chapel, praying, and asking God to help him with his inner journey. He regularly walked the perimeter of the prison, and prayed and reflected on his life.

Then one day, he felt a surge of power that came from deep within himself. It was a divine gift—a new sense of knowing. Chris said, "For the first time, I knew I was a good person, and I knew I was truly a child of God. The doubts were over. I suddenly knew who I was."

It changed his life.

Chris accepted the gift of self-esteem, and made it his own. He didn't slink around anymore. He walked with confidence. Even though a physical prisoner, he was psychologically and spiritually free for the first time in his life. Ironic, isn't it? A prisoner, and yet free for the first time. This new knowing and acceptance of himself changed the way he felt, the way he saw himself, the way he talked, and especially how he saw his life—his new reality.

When the long-awaited day of release came, Chris faced the future with joy mixed with fear. Despite his fears, he landed a good job, sorted out his life, and built better relationships, including a relationship with his two boys.

Taking the inward journey had freed Chris to love and accept himself. Then, he was able to make changes in other areas of his life.

Our second engagement on the inward journey is our relationship with God. God and His Kingdom are within us, and we venture inward to discover Him. God reveals Himself through our self, yet He is not our self. Rather, God is a separate force and entity. He speaks through our consciousness, but He is not our consciousness.

This engagement with God will take us deep into the quiet places of the soul to meet the Spirit. This journey makes us sensitive to God's whisper.

Knowing ourselves is the first step to knowing the Infinite One of Eternity. Do you feel the excitement of getting to know yourself, and getting to know God? The excitement of your pursuit will motivate you inward, forward, and upward!

There is no substitute for the inward journey. It is your responsibility alone. The insights you gain on this incredible adventure will be invaluable.

Questions to Ponder:

1. Have you taken the inward journey?
2. Do you still have more work to do on your inward journey?
3. What have you learned about yourself? About your relationship with God?

Psychological Insight

The inward journey is necessary for success in life. Everything we learn will help us love and accept ourselves. God is as eager as we are to have this happen!

He Taught Us to Focus

"You can't depend on your eyes when your life and view of God is out of focus."

Ten-year-old Johnny was challenged by his teacher to recite the preamble to the Constitution without interruption. If he could do it, his teacher promised to treat him to a scoop of ice cream, in the flavor of his choice.

Johnny began with tremendous vigor, rattling off Jefferson's words with great rapidity. Halfway through his assignment, without missing a word—he quickly slipped in "Was that a single scoop or a double?" Then, without catching his breath, he continued to the last word. Without realizing he had lost, he confidently finished and said, "strawberry."

Johnny got an "A" for effort, an "F" for focus.

When it comes to focusing on life, many of us have an attention deficit. We are easily distracted from what we claim is most significant in our lives.

Jesus was intensely focused. It says, "he set his face to go to Jerusalem."[4] Jerusalem was the place where He would give His life so others could gain eternal life through Him. Going to Jerusalem was the heart of Jesus' mission. It was there He knew He would complete His life's work. It was for this purpose He came into the arena of human life.

Focus is one of the most significant tools for psychological success and happiness. We see that when Jesus was focused on His path and direction, He saw it with distinctiveness and clarity. His mission and goal in life was where His energy and His interest were directed. He was completely focused on His task.

Without focus, we approach life, relationships and our work half-heartedly. Then, we stand back and wonder why we have half-hearted results! Deep within our hearts, however, we know why! The unwritten principle of God's Kingdom is that, in life, we receive in direct proportion to what we give.

One of my favorite stories is about a man who sought wisdom. He went to the hills, where he was told there was a wise old man who could help him. After finding the old man, the younger asked "What virtue must I possess to obtain wisdom in my life?"

To his surprise, the old man sat, silent and motionless. The young man repeated the question, but the man continued to be silent. Finally, the old man rose to his feet and motioned the young man to follow. The old man came to a pond and waded into the water up to his waist. He beckoned the young man to follow him. Puzzled by the old man's actions, yet afraid to disobey, he waded out to his mentor.

The old man suddenly seized him and pushed him under the water. He held him under the water for what seemed like an eternity. When he was finally released, the young man gasped bitterly "Why did you do this to me?" Calmly, the wise man walked to shore. He sat down again, and then he spoke. "My son, when you want wisdom in your life as much as you wanted that breath of fresh air, you will find it!"

Imagine what gifts await us if we focus on the things we want in life as much as we want the next breath of air!

The purpose of focus is to start a task, to work on it, then to bring the task to completion.

It is the completion that is highly significant. In my work with my clients, and in my personal life, I find that you can have a weak beginning and still finish strong. Think of the tortoise and the hare! Those who are most focused on their own healing and persistent in working toward it are the ones who will find wholeness in their own lives.

When James came to see me, he was completely scattered in his thoughts and actions. He was proud of being a self-described "jack of all trades, and a master of none." Yet, as we talked, it was clear that he was overwhelmed. His scattered energy was wasted on too many efforts.

James began to realize how not mastering anything in life was impacting him negatively. He didn't do anything well! He decided to focus on what he wanted to accomplish in life, and get rid of other distractions. Once he implemented his decision, his life improved, and he was much happier.

James learned there is no substitute for focus.

In his book, *The 7 Habits of Highly Effective People,* Stephen Covey writes that we often focus on the immediate and the pressing, rather than on what is most important. We answer the phone because its ring irritates us. We are distracted by false urgencies. The small and the petty things in life hinder us from working on the bigger picture. This breaks our focus and stifles our energy, and we fail to reach our goals.

In my own life, I notice that my focus often becomes weak. I might be working on a significant project, and I take a telephone call. Or I go to the mailbox instead of working at my desk. Someone stops to chat for a few minutes, and I stop to listen. I am continually reminding myself to focus.

I once asked the president of the graduate school I was attending if he would speak at a men's retreat I was sponsoring. He quickly said "no," and I was offended. He explained what his responsibilities at the school were what prevented him from coming, but I still didn't understand. Years later, I realize that he was sharing with me one of his secrets of success. He wanted to stay totally focused on his work. Because of his focus, he has received many rewards.

Jesus was totally focused. By modeling this for us, He gives us a valuable psychological insight for life! Energy always follows focus. What we choose to focus on will expand and grow

I love Classic Cars. I especially love early-model Mustangs. I would often look at the Classic Car section of the Detroit News, and usually find a Mustang listed. Before I knew it, I would have the phone in my hand! Then I would take a trip out to view another special car. By the time Monday rolled around, I would be trying to financially juggle my budget to afford another Mustang. My focus expanded from just reading the classifieds to putting energy into what I was focusing on—the car. Here's what this looks like:

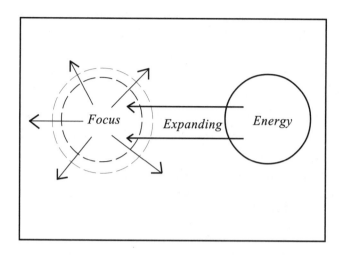

Looking at this chart, it's easy to understand why focusing on negative thoughts, things or ideas is so dangerous in our lives. If we focus on them, they will expand! Lack of focus, as well as focusing on the wrong things, sabotages our spiritual and psychological well-being.

When Jesus shared with his closest associates the object of His focus, to go to Jerusalem and give His life for others, they became alarmed. Peter took Jesus aside and tried to talk Him out of going. The text tells us "But turning and looking at His disciples, He rebuked Peter and said,"[5] Get behind me, Satan! For you are setting your mind not on divine things, but human things." Sharp words! Not only did Jesus rebuke Peter, He also turned and rebuked His other disciples for trying to break His focus. But Jesus wasn't going to leave the success of His personal mission to another person, or a committee.

In the Gospel of Matthew, [6]we find that Peter had a problem with focus. Peter was impressed when he saw Jesus walking on the water, and was invited by Jesus to do the same. Peter's focus on Jesus allowed him to make it a certain distance across the water—it took him to a place he had never been before. Yet Peter lost his focus. He noticed the strong wind, and became frightened and began to sink. He cried out "Lord, save me!"[7] Jesus reached out His hand, and Peter was saved.

Peter broke his concentration. The darkened sky, the rising waves splashing up against his legs, and the fierce wind beating against his face all caused him to focus on the storm, and not Jesus. Peter, as many of us often are, was overwhelmed by the storms of life and lost his focus on the power of God.

When we lose our focus, we will always sink. When we sustain our focus, we will reap rewards that we would otherwise have not received if we had strayed from our original path.

Questions to Ponder:

1. How many projects have you started, and then lost your focus?
2. What types of things cause you to lose your focus?
3. Beginning right now, decide what you need to focus on and bring to completion.

Psychological Insight

Focus on what is significant in your life. Remember, as you stay focused, you will be blessed with dividends along the way.

He Taught That It Is Up to Us

"Believe in your strength and your vision. Learn to repeat it to yourself, 'It all depends on me.' " Andre Gide

Janet and her husband Brian came to my office faithfully for six months, trying to patch up their marriage. Both were ready to call it quits. Like many couples, Janet and Brian knew how to work together and how to play together, but not how to fight fairly. They were "fighting on every hill" rather than deciding "what hill to fight on." Consequently, their marriage relationship majored on the minors. They constantly battled about the wrong issues.

Janet came from a home with a difficult father who would not allow her to express her opinions. He would often walk away from her in the middle of a conversation. Every time Brian got quiet and walked away from a dispute, she panicked and replayed her childhood experience. Desperately, she would chase Brian, and stand between him and the door to prevent him from leaving. Her fear of rejection was tremendously frightening to Janet.

Brian tried to explain to Janet that when he walked away, he needed a break. He was not abandoning her. He needed to go to "his cave" and think things over, and cool off.

I gave Janet and Brian some guidelines for confronting each other fairly:

- One fight at a time.
- No gunny sacking (pulling old unresolved issues out of the bag).
- No bringing other people into the confrontation.
- Stay in the present tense.
- Ask what you want out of the confrontation.
- Discuss how to resolve the dispute.
- Try to understand what the other person is feeling.
- Take responsibility for what you may be doing wrong.
- No button pushing.
- No put-downs, or name calling.
- If necessary, allow your partner a "time out."
- Stick to the issues. Don't wander off.
- Listen to what the other person is saying, even if you don't agree with it.
- Don't let the problem go unsolved.

Janet began to give Brian space in their disputes, without the abusive behavior she had displayed earlier. Brian promised Janet that he would always come back to work on the problem and resolve it with her. Their relationship improved, and they were both encouraged.

At their next appointment, Brian began thanking me for saving their marriage. But it was credit for success I hadn't earned. I told him, "Brian, I may have given you the tools, but you took them and used them. Brian and Janet, it's all up to you!"

The heart of therapy is not the power that is in the hands of the therapist, but the power that is in the hands of those who seeks to be healed. The hard work of change is up to them!

In my own experience, many of my clients literally die of thirst at the foot of the well in rigor mortis. Some are in denial. Others are slaves to their own egos. Whatever the reason, unable to change—death still comes.

Jesus told us many times that it is up to us to change. If you want something good to happen in your life; if you want to see a door opened; if you want a mountain moved; if you want to walk; if you want a vision; if you want to be forgiven; it's up to you to make it happen.

Jesus did not leave it up to our imaginations to figure out the dynamics of this significant psychological and spiritual key. It boils down to faith, that personal ingredient that is ours and ours alone. Faith is like a bath—no one can take it for you! Faith is the door that opens life's opportunities and possibilities to us. What happens or doesn't happen to you is most likely in direct proportion to your faith.

The word "faith" was frequently on the lips of Jesus. He appeared to judge everything by faith. The success of your own psychological well-being will depend on your faith, faith in yourself and faith in God. Jesus compared faith to the tiniest seed in the land of Galilee—the mustard seed. Jesus says "For truly, if you have the faith the grain of a mustard seed you will say to this mountain, 'Move hence to yonder place, and it will move; and nothing will be impossible to you.'"[8] Jesus told a woman who came to Him "O woman, great is your faith! Be it done for you as you desire."[9] She was healed instantly.

When Peter was sinking in the waves, Jesus reached out His hand and caught him, saying, "O man of little faith, why did you doubt?"[10] Jesus also told a woman who had hemorrhaged for 12 years, and pushed against Him in the crowd, hoping to touch His garment and be healed, to "Take heart, your faith has made you well."

One of the most moving stories in the New Testament is that of Lazarus, a man Jesus loved. I believe he was like a brother to Jesus. In the story, we find that Lazarus has died, and it takes several days for Jesus to reach his sisters Mary and Martha, who are weeping in grief. Jesus also weeps at the loss of His friend. Jesus said "Did I not tell you that if you would believe you would see the glory of God?" Then he prays, and calls out with a loud voice, "Lazarus, come out." New life surges in Lazarus' limp, dead body. They unbind him from his grave clothes, and let him go, alive and whole.[11]

In Biblical narrative, we read of two blind men who follow Jesus, asking to receive sight. Jesus reverses the process he used with Mary and Martha, and asks the two men if they believe He is able to restore their vision. Immediately, both men reply, "Yes, Lord." He touches their eyes, saying "According to your faith, let it be done to you." They go away healed, rejoicing and praising God.[12]

In each story, faith makes the difference. Without faith, each story would have ended in tragedy. Without faith, each individual would have stayed in their misery, untouched by the love of God. It is their faith, and their active participation in the process of healing, that is what Jesus says makes the difference. Jesus blessed their "yes."

To us today, He is still saying "It is up to you."

Faith affects our attitude, outlook and behavior. Not only is it a rational decision to have faith, it is also an emotional response. The first part of faith is the confident belief that something we want is going to happen. The second part of faith is an active participation in the process of growth and healing. Faith is a way of living and seeing the world. Faith is also an attempt to see the world as God sees it. Faith is a total response of our hearts, minds and souls.

Faith is also like a bridge. Its support structure is buried deep below the surface, unseen. Yet, it is there with great strength, holding us up in times of difficulty.

In the Bible, the word "faith" appears over 748 times. Jesus said that faith is the difference between nothing happening and a miracle. If you want a miracle, Jesus declares, then you need to believe it can happen! Jesus said, "believe that what you say will come to pass, it will be done to you."[13]

Here's what the formula looks like:

DESIRE + FAITH - DOUBT = SUCCESS

However, faith is much more than a definition, a formula, or a therapeutic tool to make us feel good. It is an active, dynamic, experience of internal decisions, a series of saying "yes," which give us a way to operate every day. Faith keeps us in contact with ourselves and especially with God. Faith is also like a muscle; the more we use it, the stronger it becomes, and the greater our possibilities. Faith is uniquely personal.

You might ask, "How do faith and psychology fit together?" Good question! I believe our mind, body, and spirit all function in harmony. There is no sharp division; no neat but separate categories. For many years, hospitals clearly separated spiritual beliefs from medical treatment. I remember, as a minister, visiting patients in the hospital and being treated as a nuisance and insignificant to the recovery of the patient! Today, this is changing. Hospitals are built with chapels for meditation, and prayer is often acknowledged as part of the healing process. Belief has become a key ingredient in treatment.

What a delight it would be if every person who needs help would come with a framework of knowing and believing in themselves! It would change the impact of every experience. It would change the outcome of every experience. It would change the seeker!

Jesus says the power is already there, waiting for you to use. The faith is up to you. He is reaching across time that separates us from Him and asking, as he asked the blind man, "Do you believe I can do this?" The blind man said "Yes!"[14] What is your answer?

Questions to Ponder:

1. On a scale of zero to ten, with ten as the highest, how would you rate your personal faith?

2. How has your faith grown over the last five years? What has helped it grow?

3. Through faith, what would you like to see happen in your life?

Psychological Insight

Faith is the personal ingredient that can unlock everything good in your life. Jesus is clear; the decision to have faith rests on you! He is standing by, waiting to do His part. The power and healing is set aside as God's gift to you. Believe in Him who says all things are possible!

He Had Purpose in His Life

"The world in which we live is divine destiny. There is a divine meaning in the life of every individual and of you and me."
—Martin Buber, I and Thou (1952)

Sal was my best friend when I was in college. But Sal had a problem—he didn't know what he wanted to do with his life. Everyone in my social group knew exactly what they wanted to do, and were preparing for it. Except Sal.

Sometimes, as we walked to classes, Sal would talk to me about how difficult his lack of purpose was for him. He was frustrated and floundering, not knowing what courses to take and what direction he was headed in. He felt as if he was wasting his time, and he wasn't paying attention in class, or giving anything his best effort. Consequently, his grades were poor.

After his second year of college, Sal dropped out. He discovered an aptitude for communications, which he enjoyed, and became very successful in the field of radio.

There's an old saying, "Aim at nothing, and you are sure to hit it." Having purpose in life changes everything.

Jesus had purpose! His purpose was at the heart of His view of life. He knew why He had come, what He wanted to do and how He wanted to do it. He said "I must proclaim the good news of the kingdom of God to the other cities also, for I was sent for this purpose."[15] In the garden, before He went to the Cross, we read in John 12:27-28 that He said, "No, it is for this purpose I have come to this hour. Father, glorify Your name."[16]

Purpose allows us to focus our life, to harness our energy, to pay attention to what we deem to be important, and to stay focused until we complete our task.

Purpose gives us a reason to get up in the morning, a reason to work during the day, and a reason to lay our head down at night. Purpose makes our life worthwhile. It gives life meaning.

We do not know at what moment in His life Jesus knew who He was and what His purpose was, but we do know at the age of twelve He was already focused on what He perceived to be His mission. On their way back from Jerusalem, Mary and Joseph found that their son Jesus was missing from the caravan. Racing back to Jerusalem, they found Jesus conversing with the learned men in the Temple, who were amazed at Jesus' knowledge!

Jesus told his parents matter-of-factly, [17]"Did you not know I must be about my father's business?". Even at this early age, Jesus was driven by His purpose in life. He never let anyone deter Him from it.

When we know our purpose, we do not have to waste time and energy on meaningless movement. We are like a beam of light focused in a specific direction.

In his book, *Man's Search For Meaning,* Vicktor Frankl makes an interesting observation about purpose. Frankl was a Jewish psychiatrist captured by the Germans in 1943 and imprisoned at Auschwitz, a concentration camp. Fifteen hundred prisoners were cramped into a shed that was meant to house two hundred people. As he endured the horrific conditions day after day, he observed that many who gave up and died in the camp were some of the strongest prisoners, while many of the physically frail and weak survived. Frankl pondered over the key to this phenomenon, and finally discovered the answer. Those who survived the grotesque circumstances of prison life had something to live for, a purpose for the future. They knew there was a task waiting for them to fulfill. Nietzche once said, "He who has a why to live for can bear almost any how." Where there is purpose, there is life!

Without purpose, we are like a ship without a rudder, driven by the mercy of the waves. Purpose pushes us moment by moment, day by day, to keep working when others quit. Purpose inspires us and gives us hope.

Jesus had purpose from the beginning of His life to the end. He began by saying He must be doing the work of His Father. On the Cross, He uttered, "It is finished!" With His last breath, He completed the task for which He stepped foot upon the earth. In the days that followed, He ascended to His Father where He rules in anticipation of coming again.

Do you know what your purpose in life is? Everyone has a unique purpose. We may not be a Princess Diana or a Ghandi or even a Mother Theresa. You may be called to be a husband, a wife, a parent, a son or a daughter. Your purpose may be as simple as baking apple pies, giving kind words to strangers, lending a listening ear to someone in need, or praying on behalf of a child. Our purpose may be ordinary, rather than great or extraordinary. Yet we must have purpose to live a successful life. The key to finding your purpose is being an instrument of God's peace wherever you are!

My son Tom achieved financial success following his graduation, working as a specialist in the field of environmental waste. The business world was good to Tom, and he surrounded himself with a lot of toys: four boats, two snowmobiles, and several cars—all at the same time!

But Tom knew something was missing. One morning, he woke up and said to himself, "I'm successful, but this is not my purpose in life!" He talked it over with his wife Sue, and Tom began searching his heart for his true purpose. He decided what he really wanted to do was become a teacher. With the full support of Sue, they worked out a budget that would allow him to go back to school and still support her and his three children. This meant Tom's many toys were sold to afford tuition, books, and basic necessities for his family.

Tom began by teaching "at risk" children in the Michigan school system. His class was composed of kids who are repeated troublemakers, and on the borderline of being permanently expelled. From there he accepted a position in the high school teaching kids geography. Today, he makes less money, works longer hours and his job is more difficult. But is he happier? "Yes!" Tom says. "This is the purpose for which I was born, this is where I belong."

When you find purpose in your life, you can live with less and feel you have much more!

Questions to Ponder:

1. What is your purpose in life?
2. How does your purpose give your life meaning?
3. Are you living out your purpose?

Psychological Insight

Without purpose, we have no direction in our lives. Find your purpose for your life as early in life as possible. Stick to it, and don't get sidetracked by distractions. Remember your direction may change as your purpose is redefined.

He Said to Keep the Child Alive

"When asked what accounted for his success, Albert Einstein replied that he never grew up, and always saw the world through the eyes of a child."

Jim sits across from me on the green couch in my office. It's an intense session. His eyes are closed, and tears are streaming down his cheeks. In his mind, he is recounting a scene from his childhood that often plagues him.

"What do you see, Jim?" I ask.

"My mother and father are arguing, and my father is about to hit my mother."

"Where are you, where is little Jimmy?" I continue.

"I'm standing between my mother and father. I'm telling my father that if he hurts my mother, I'm going to kill him. My father is angry, and slaps me to the floor."

Jim continues with the story of a twelve-year-old boy who is hurt, and trying to intervene to help his mother. He remembers crawling to the corner of the kitchen and trying to recover from the blow his father dealt him. Jim is crying now, and in a fetal position on my couch.

"Relax, Jim, that situation cannot hurt you anymore. You're okay," I repeat several times.

Jim relaxes for a moment, and sighs in relief.

"Jim, you're an adult now. What do you want to say to Jimmy?" I say.

Jim tells "little Jimmy" that he is coming to help him, and that he is going to be okay. Then there is a silence. This session was over, but I knew it was one of many visits. Jim would have to go"back to the future" to heal his inner wounded child."

Perhaps one of the greatest breakthroughs that has occurred in our time is a new understanding of the inner child. We now know that if the inner child has been wounded during a developmental stage that we have the capability to go back and to heal. The well-being of us as adults greatly depends on the health of our inner child.

The Great Psychologist gives a stern warning against abusing His children. Indeed, He says it would be better to put a millstone around your neck and drown in the sea!

Children were very important to Jesus. One time in his ministry, as He was teaching the people, several adults brought their children to Him, asking for Him to lay His hands on them and to bless them. His disciples, were upset by this development, and stepped in to prevent them from reaching Jesus. They tried to push the parents and their children away. When Jesus discovered what was going on, He told the disciples to "cool it!" Then He used the moment to teach the adults a valuable lesson about His Kingdom.

Jesus set a child in the midst of the people and declared in Mark 10:15, "Unless you become like a little child you cannot enter the Kingdom of God."[18] Another time, He taught that we must humble ourselves as a child. He said there are three ways we need to treat children:

· We are to welcome and accept children.

· We are to be careful not to cause any child to stumble who believes in God

· We are not to despise any of these little ones.

Children can teach us many things about life and the eternal kingdom of God. Experts on angels believe that children come from God, and retain a small measure of memory of their existence with God before they were born. Consequently, children are receptive, intuitive, and aware of spiritual experiences occurring around them.

A woman at my seminar on angels told me how she and her three-year-old daughter Amy were looking at a book together. Amy pointed to a picture and said, "Look, mom! That's an angel." The surprised mother asked how she knew about angels. Amy told her that when she was a little baby and very sick, the angels would come and sing to her.

Perhaps children see reality better than adults!

A child has several gifts worth possessing as adults. Some of these include:

· TOTAL DEPENDENCY: The child looks to the parent for food, shelter, clothing and love. If the child doesn't get it, he suffers and dies. The child cannot get what he needs on his own.

· INNOCENCE: There is something beautiful about the innocence of a child. They are pure and without contamination. They see the world as uncontaminated by evil, and having a clean heart.

· TRUST: How often does a small child come to us with a broken toy, believing that we can fix it? When she is older, she brings us her broken dreams for us to fix. Yet, somewhere between childhood and adulthood, we lose this simple faith.

· HUMILITY: Jesus specifically mentions this as a virtue. A child is authentic and unpretentious. Adults often try to be someone they are not!

· LOVE: This is one of the most powerful virtues in a child. One of our main tasks as adults is to teach a child to love. Children have a great capacity for it! In therapy, I have seen children protect and excuse unloving, abusive, parents because they love them so much. This love is as close to being unconditional as it can be this side of heaven.

· BELIEF IN FANTASY: A child believes all things are possible! Animals can talk, and elephants can fly. Children have exciting imaginations, and we may feel their "make-believe world" is naïve, but they haven't been poisoned by the cynicism of adults.

· FORGIVENESS: Children fight and then make up with each other quickly. Adults tend to bear grudges for a long time! Perhaps a child forgives easily because it has not experienced broken promises and lies. However, Jesus made it clear that forgiveness is a key ingredient in the life of a believer. Don't expect to receive forgiveness if you haven't given it to others.

Difficult experiences in life will come like a thief to rob us and profane the divine gifts inherent in the child, and seek to destroy them. Those who wreak this destruction will have a great price to pay.

Jesus stated that unless we become as little children, we will not be healthy enough to enter the kingdom of God. Regardless of our age, we still have a "little child within." If that child is damaged or impaired as we mature, we will be unhealthy adults. Modern psychology tells us to discover the child within, and to keep it alive and heal it, if necessary.

Jesus was ahead of His time in understanding the value of the child, and the child within us. It would be well for us to respect the wisdom of the Great Psychologist, and honor children, encourage their growth and well-being, and understand how their virtues are worth possessing.

Our challenge is to never surrender these characteristics regardless of our age. We need to give up what is *childish*, and retain what is *childlike*. How wonderful it would be to be more playful, authentic, and take life a little more lightly! We need to laugh, to love, to forgive, and to truly believe.

Not a bad way to travel through life!

Questions to Ponder:

1. Are you in touch with your inner child?

2. Is your inner child healthy? If so, what characteristics of a child do you possess?

3. What child in your life needs your attention? Name some ways you will address this.

Psychological Insight

Understand the wonderful characteristics of children, and implement as many of those characteristics in your own life as you can—regardless of your age! Get in touch with and heal your own wounded inner child. Approach the Great Psychologist as His child.

He Taught Us to Work Through Our Fears

"You gain strength, courage and confidence by every experience in which you stop to look fear in the face."
—Eleanor Roosevelt

We are facing an epidemic of fear in our contemporary society. Our homes, our cities, our streets and even the playgrounds of our schools have become bloody battlefields of violence. Personal safety has become an all-consuming issue in the minds of many Americans.

My clients often are gripped by fear. They fear new beginnings, as well as endings. They fear failure, and—surprisingly—they fear success. They fear cancer, AIDS, and other diseases. Sometimes, they don't even know what they fear.

Such fears, real or imaginary, lead us to psychological and emotional rigor mortis. For those with codependent backgrounds, there is a fear of rejection and abandonment.

These two powerfully devastating and crippling experiences may be connected to a specific event which sparked a particular fear. For some, just the thought of rejection or abandonment may plague an individual's relationships.

Shirley was such an individual. In her first marriage, Shirley dreaded confronting her husband John. For many years, she buried her feelings and lived in silent misery in her unhappiness. One night, she mustered up the courage to speak to her husband, who worked the afternoon shift and got home late. For hours, she lay awake in the dark, dreading the moment John would arrive home. Around midnight, she heard John's key in the door. John and Shirley exchanged the usual greetings and he began undressing for bed. Tentatively, Shirley began telling him that she was unhappy in their relationship. John paused in his undressing. Shirley continued to explain, and asked John to go to marriage counseling with her.

John turned on the bedroom light, pulled his suitcase out of the closet, and began stuffing his clothes into it, despite Shirley's tearful protests. Then he left. A week later he filed for divorce.

Shirley's fear of abandonment and rejection was now a reality, and will impact all of her future relationships.

Fear creates a ghetto for most of us. When we traditionally think of a ghetto, we think of a physical place in a city where a particular ethnic group is restricted to live. When I grew up in New York City in the 1940s, different blocks were characterized by different nationalities. My brother would warn against going into a different neighborhood of a different ethnic group.

The ghetto I speak about here is the ghetto of the human mind and heart. It is more confining than a physical ghetto, because a mental ghetto is something you always take with you. Such a confinement not only limits our opportunities, but also the way we see the world.

We create these ghettos ourselves. They hold us captive, regardless of our social status, ethnic background, or bank account. You cannot buy yourself out of a mental ghetto. Our minds build the strongest prisons!

How long have you been in your ghetto? How did you get there? What keeps you imprisoned in your ghetto?

Jesus was not afraid of ghettos. He often entered them to share His principles of truth and freedom to those who were captive either physically or psychologically. No ghetto was able to confine Him. He always invited others to climb out of their ghettos.

When we are imprisoned in the ghetto of fear, we may end up getting exactly what we are afraid of. One of my patients, Scott, was afraid of rejection. Despite being good looking and successful in his work, Scott had never had a meaningful relationship. In his last two relationships, the woman had ended it, much to Scott's pain and agony. He believed that women could not be trusted, and these two rejections confirmed this for him.

What Scott feared, he received, again and again.

Although Scott was obviously getting what he feared, he needed to understand his part in shaping a destiny he claimed he did not want. In each relationship, Scott never fully committed to the woman he was involved with. He held his emotions and feelings in check for fear of rejection. Consequently, the woman would sense this and build walls to protect herself. One of his girlfriends, Marcia, was so afraid of the rejection she sensed from Scott that she walked away, fearful of an even bigger rejection if she allowed the relationship to go any further.

It is not until we move into our fear that we have the greatest potential to understand it and to conquer it. If we do not conquer our fear, it will conquer us.

I have battled fears of my own. When I accepted a job in downtown Detroit at the Penobscot Building several years ago, I was both elated and anxious. My new office was on the 22nd floor of the building, and I was afraid of elevators.

First, I decided to walk up the stairway to work. Then I found out they were inaccessible for daily use. Frustrated, I said to myself, "Enough is enough! I am forty-nine years old, and this is ridiculous." I decided to conquer my fear. When the elevator door opened that first day, I was nervous and reluctant, but I got on it and made it to my office. By the end of the second day, I was feeling more at ease. I told myself I could handle it. For two years, I daily worked on my fear.

Jesus was no stranger to fear! Before His death, He was deeply troubled. After supping with His disciples, they withdrew to the ravine of Kedron where there was a garden. He separated Himself from them, and went to pray alone. His fear was so intense, His sweat was like drops of blood! In Luke 22:42, we read that He asked "Father, if Thou art willing, remove this cup from me." Jesus, a man of flesh and blood, felt fear. Yet he did not run from it!

As Jesus prayed, we read in Luke 22:43 that an angel suddenly appeared without warning. There is a famous painting depicting this event, with the angel hugging the exhausted Jesus. I have often wondered what the angel said to Jesus. Perhaps, "Your Father loves you. Don't be discouraged. You can do it!"

That night Jesus acknowledged His fear, and stepped forward to meet it with the words found in Gospel of Matthew "My Father if this cannot pass unless I drink it, Your will be done."[21] It took the courage of action to utter these words! Jesus confronted His fear.

It is not until we confront our fears that we have the greatest potential to understand and conquer them. The famous movie star, Chuck Norris, as a teenager remembers being chased by a bully. Norris' boss at the gas station where he worked saw this happening, and said sternly to him, "Chuck, someday you will have to stop running." This was a turning point for Norris! He decided to face his fear, and soon moved beyond it.

Jesus, the Great Psychologist, faced the depths of His fears. He stepped forward to meet them, with His cross in His hand, and said, "I can handle this." It didn't change the cruel beating He received at the hands of the Romans. It didn't change His crucifixion. It did change how He viewed what was happening to Him and how He felt about it!

There comes a time when we must face our fears. Our belief by itself won't make them disappear. Did the Biblical David feel fear as he stepped out to meet Goliath, the giant in his life? Certainly! But David refused to be immobilized by his fear. He believed in himself, and in God. David kept facing his fears until they were just meaningless putty. In 1 Samuel 17, we read how with the throw of a stone, the threatening giant in his life lay helpless on the floor of the valley. How ironic! This was a giant that had paralyzed the entire Israelite army. When we confront our fears, or giants, the giant may fall more easily than we expect!

When we understand our fear and its source and refuse to let it stop us, refuse to let it immobilize us, and refuse to let it stop our positive thinking, we will conquer our fear.

Jesus' teachings will not make our fears go away. Rather, His teachings will help us know what to do when fear comes knocking on our door.

Face your fears head-on, and persevere.

Questions to Ponder

1. Take an inventory of your fears. What are you struggling with the most?
2. How can you face these fears?
3. Choose one fear, and begin confronting it today. Ask a friend to hold you accountable.

Psychological Insight

Understand your fears. Don't run from them. Face your fears, and you will ultimately conquer them.

He Knew Himself

"Every human being is intended to have a character of his own; to be what no other is, and to do what no other can do."
—William Channing

Homer Hickam Jr. had a dream of building rockets. Yet Homer's father had other plans for him. Homer's father wanted him to work in the coal mines in Coalwood, West Virginia, just as he and Homer's grandfather had done. His father claimed he knew who his son was and what he should do with his life. "One day, if you want to, you could even take over my job as superintendent at the mine," Homer Sr. told his son. If Homer would follow his father's dream for his life, he would please his parent.

Through the encouragement of his science teacher, Miss Riley, Homer didn't give up his dream of building rockets—and making something of himself. Homer befriended Quentin, the smartest kid in school but a class outcast. With two other friends, he formed the Big Creek Missile Agency Rocket Club.

The bestselling book, *October Skies,* chronicles the numerous trials and errors the boys experienced as they experimented with rocket fuel and nozzle sizes. The first rocket blew up part of the white picket fence around Homer's home. Other rockets disintegrated when they were launched. But the boys persevered. They entered the local science fair—and ended up winning the National Science Fair. Thirty-one rockets later, a group of 600 coal miners and parents watched as Homer's "Auk XXX1" took off, flying nearly six miles straight up into the open sky.

What a dream for a high school student in the 1950s, especially in this mining town where young people seldom went to college! Homer lived out his dream, graduating from college and working for NASA as an engineer. In 1997, the Shuttle Columbia carried a piece of the nozzle from one of Homer's rockets and his science fair medal into space.

Homer never forgot who he was, even though others tried to define who he was and what he should do. Homer reached deep within himself and believed in himself.

At Caesarea Phillippi, Jesus asked His disciples who people said He was. The disciples, who had been listening to people talk, answered "John the Baptist, Elijah, Jeremiah or one of the prophets of old." Jesus then asked, "But who do you say that I am?"

It was Peter who answered, "You are the Messiah, the Son of the living God."[22] Jesus was pleased by this revelation, but then He did a mysterious thing. He sternly ordered them not to tell anyone that He was the Messiah.

Why?

There were many misconceptions the Jews had about the coming Messiah. Jesus saw these misconceptions, and deemed them to be traps that would hinder His work.

Here are some of the misconceptions about the Messiah:

- · He would be a military leader, who would gather an army and attempt to overthrow the Romans
- · He would be a political leader
- · He would be a religious leader, enforcing the literal letter of the law
- · He would be a king, and establish a kingdom on the earth.

All of these ideas define what the Messiah was expected to be, and what role people expected Jesus to play. But Jesus was the master of His own destiny. He knew the pitfalls of allowing others to define who He was and what He should do in His life. He refused to go in a destructive direction. He defined who He was and is, and what He would do in His lifetime. He knew He was the Son of God, the Messiah, the Christ, and while He allowed others to use such titles to describe Him, in general He avoided using them to describe Himself. It wasn't that these truths weren't valid. Jesus didn't want unreal expectations, popular opinion, and even myth to define Him.

Consequently, Jesus deliberately chose His own title to define who He believed Himself to be and what title best portrayed His work. He calls Himself the "Son of Man."[23] This title best defines who He was, is, and how He saw Himself during His time on earth. This title is not used by disciples or followers of Jesus, only Jesus Himself.

Who was this Son of Man? In the Book of Daniel, the Son of Man is a mysterious angelic figure who appears to be the fulfillment of God's kingdom here on earth. In Isaiah 53, the Son of Man is a suffering servant who comes in the name of the Lord, but faces humiliation at the end of time to be a judge to Israel. Jesus is one who suffers, one who serves, one who will face humiliation, and one who will be God's judge.

There is always someone in our life who wants to define who we are and who they think we should be. As a teenager, I remember working with my grandfather in a fruit market in Grand Rapids, Michigan. Grandpa took care of the produce department, and I stocked the grocery shelves. One day, as we were working, Grandpa asked me what I wanted to do with my life. He laughed when I told him I wanted to go to college.

"What's so funny?" I asked him, puzzled by his laughter.

"Only smart kids go to college," Grandpa said, seriously.

"Well, I'm smart," I said, defending myself, trying to hide my hurt.

"You're the only one who thinks so!" was his caustic reply. He walked away laughing, leaving me puzzled and hurt. After all these years, I can still hear his words. Fortunately, the sting is gone.

My grandfather's view of me was limited. Fortunately, I didn't completely subscribe to his view of me. But, there were more challenges ahead. Not a single one of my family members had ever gone to college more than a year. There was no financial help from my family. Whatever I did about furthering my schooling, I would have to pioneer myself. I remember leaving for college, and saying goodbye to my father. He complained to me that he had just lost $550 at the track. I was stunned and hurt, and tried my best to hide it. In my pocket was $585, all the money I had saved for a year of schooling. Tears ran down my face as I left him.

I was determined to prove my grandfather wrong. His words spurred me on through college, and became a monkey on my back. Even when he passed away during my college years, I became more determined to make it. The monkey on my back was a motivator.

The day I graduated, I crossed the platform at Hope College, grasped my diploma and said in my heart, "Look at this, Grandpa! Only smart kids go to college. Well, you were wrong about me!" My smile was the biggest in the college chapel, and it lasted a long, long, time.

After earning two more degrees, I am glad I listened to the voice within me, and not my Grandpa. Don't let anyone define who you are, or what you can be. You tell them who you are! You tell them what you will do, and then do it! Don't settle for anything less. The price you will pay if you settle for less is too high. Make the monkeys on your back your motivators. Take the words that others use to hinder you from reaching your goals, and use them to push yourself to your goals.

Questions to Ponder:

1. Have you defined who you are? Describe yourself in a few sentences.

2. Who around you has tried to redefine who you are?

3. Do you have a monkey on your back? How can you change the monkey to a motivator?

Psychological Insight

One of the most significant gifts you can give yourself is knowing who you are. Be authentic. Stay away from those who will not allow you to be who you are. Define yourself, rather than let others define you.

He Asked for What He Wanted

"He who would be well taken care of must take care of himself."
—William Sumner

Jennifer was unhappy in her marriage. As I listened to her during her appointment, I found that this was a recurring theme in all of her relationships. However, I was not surprised by this. Jennifer came from a home where she did not feel valued. Jennifer's father ruled the family with old-fashioned, German strictness, and was the only one allowed to be angry. Her older brother, John, received copious attention as the first-born, and her younger sister, Julie, was spoiled, and "got away with murder." When Jennifer tried to tell her parents how she felt, her mother would chastise her, telling her, "You have no right to feel that way." Jennifer learned early in life that expressing your feelings was dangerous. Whatever she felt, she stuffed down deep inside.

I encouraged Jennifer to bring in a video of her childhood, as I do with many of my clients. She chose a video of her younger sister Julie's fifth birthday party. We watched together as the camera panned from her older brother John and back to Julie, blowing out her birthday cake candles and unwrapping her gifts. Once in a while we'd get a glimpse of Jennifer somewhere between. I got dizzy following the camera back and forth from John to Julie! It never stopped on Jennifer, not even for a moment.

The video caught the relationship between Jennifer and her parents. Her parents were always focused on John or Julie, but never on Jennifer. Jennifer wanted her parent's love and attention. It was obvious that if she wanted it as an adult, she was going to have to ask for it. She would never get it by staying silent.

Asking for what you want or need is a way of taking care of yourself. No one else will do it for you. Asking is your responsibility, and yours alone.

Every day, as I counsel patients, I ask "What are you doing to take care of yourself?" Usually, the people I ask are under a lot of pressure, and have a lot of demands on them. They think their responsibility is to take care of others instead of themselves. Codependents are notorious for taking care of others while their own lives are at zero.

Taking care of yourself is important to your psychological well-being and balance. But it doesn't happen unless you ask for what you want. When you take care of yourself, and fill your life with things that make you feel good about yourself, that positive feeling will spill over to others. You feel good, others around you sense your attitude and feel good, too.

I remember counseling a woman who was overextended in her personal life, and not taking care of herself. "If you throw your husband a life preserver, and fall off the deck doing it, what value is your effort?" She looked puzzled. I continued, "When you are secure and feeling good about yourself, your efforts to help others will be more effective and you will not be running on an empty tank."

Is taking care of yourself selfish? No! Self-preservation and self-protection is a natural part of life. It's what Jesus, Ph.D., teaches us to do.

Jesus was outspoken. He called things as He saw them, and He didn't mince words. He also knew what He wanted, and wasn't afraid to ask for it. He also expected to get what He asked for. Here are some things Jesus requested:

· He asked the woman at the well for water.

· He asked His disciples to bring the little children to Him.

· He asked that His Father's house be a house of prayer.

· He asked His disciples to pray with Him in the Garden of Gethsemane.

· He asked His disciples to love one another.

· He asked His Father to keep His disciples committed to truth.

· He asked Thomas to feel His wounds.

· He asked Peter, who denied Him three times, if he truly loved Him.

The list goes on. Jesus knew the secret of taking care of Himself, and boldly asked for what He needed.

Jesus declares, "So I say to you, Ask, and it will be given to you; search, and you will find; knock, and the door will be opened for you."[24] Jesus goes on to say "For everyone who asks, receives, and everyone who searches, finds, and for everyone who knocks, the door will be opened."[25]

Not only does Jesus tell us to ask for what we want, He says we can expect to get what we want. And yet many do not unlock the psychological gifts Jesus offers. This is not just surprising, it's shocking! Yet so often we refuse the free gifts we could have. As I write these words, two lottery prizes totaling $250,000 remain unclaimed in the State of Michigan Treasury. What a waste!

Jesus, the Great Psychologist, must be saying the same thing. "What a waste!" The psychological and spiritual gifts that He promised us are set aside and available, yet they go unclaimed and unused.

Carol, a young woman I met after one of my seminars, complained to me that her husband was always more excited to see the dog and their two-year-old son when he came home from work than to see her. When he did greet her, it was unenthusiastically. She felt like the low man on the totem pole.

I asked Carol if she had ever told Jeff how she felt.

"He should know better," Carol said angrily. "We've been married five years, and he is thirty years old. I shouldn't have to ask. He should know what I need."

The solution for Carol was simple. Carol was too frightened to ask for what she needed. Yet when she shared with Jeff how she felt, he responded to her in a warm and loving way. She was miserable so many months when she didn't need to be! The longer we are married, the more important it is to remember to ask for what we want—daily. When we get used to our spouse, and take her for granted, we may forget to listen to each other and focus on our relationship.

Asking is a form of prayer. God wants us to ask Him for what we need. Asking is good for our hearts, and keeps us humble. Asking keeps us returning again and again to the source of all good gifts in life. Asking itself has therapeutic value because we are moving toward taking care of ourselves. But ask wisely. Remember not to have a shopping list of selfish demands.

Jesus emphasizes that when we ask, we will receive. Asking will lead us to life's gifts and opportunities. If you knew that what you asked for would be yours, what would you request? Don't bury your requests, ask! Then fasten your safety belt, and get ready to receive.

Questions to Ponder:

1. Do you assume others know what you need, or do you ask?
2. What have you asked for the most from God?
3. What do others ask you for the most?

Psychological Insight

Asking for what you want in life is your way of taking care of yourself. Asking God for what you want is a form of prayer. When we ask, Jesus says we will receive.

He Was in Touch with His Feelings

"You can not have psychological health without knowing what you feel, and understanding your emotions."

Many a male client has sat across from me in my office, dumbfounded, when I ask him how he feels. Even if he has several diplomas hanging on his office wall and is highly successful in the business world, he may shrug his shoulders and blurt out "I don't know!"

Men are not always aware of their feelings in our society. They are rewarded for their ability to think rationally, not for what they feel. They advance in their careers for solving problems, not simply listening to them.

Women are different in their approach to relationships. They seem to be more naturally in touch with their feelings. Men and women are so different in their approach to relationships, that it is a wonder they ever get together.

Jesus, the Great Psychologist, was a different kind of man. In His culture, men were often rigid, insensitive, and rulers of their homes. Yet Jesus was not afraid to show His emotions. Rather than seeing this as a weakness, He saw it as part of being a total man. Evidently Mary and Joseph forgot to tell Jesus not to feel too deeply, expose His feelings, and to never, never, let them see you sweat!

We are exposed to so much violence, pain, hunger, and death that we are "psychologically numb" to it. Our indifference becomes a lack of love and caring for those in our lives.

Jesus was in touch with His feelings. He knew what His feelings were, and openly expressed them to others. I believe that He laughed, He cried, He was angry, He had compassion, He showed fear, and He showed love. He showed a wide gamut of feelings without shame or embarrassment. This is what it means to be a man of the eternal kingdom, directed by the Spirit, and having the word of the Father in our hearts. This is the "new man."

The "new man" is fully alive in all of his senses and emotions. He does not try to understand people so he can love them. He loves them, and then tries to understand them. He tries to identify with the feelings of other's as well.

This is beautifully illustrated when Jesus sees a funeral procession coming out of the village of Nain. The weeping widow was bereft, for the man who died was her only son. [5]Jesus was moved by the widow's predicament, and approached the bier. He spoke gently to the woman, saying [13]"Do not weep." Then He spoke to the dead man, declaring, [14]"Young man, I say to you, rise." The young man came back to life, and Jesus handed him over to his mother, who rejoiced. Jesus felt and understood the pain of her feelings without any request from her. He had compassion. He had empathy.[26]

Jesus was fully alive emotionally. He appreciated the world in which He lived. He heard the music of life and danced to it. He experienced the beauty of life and stood in awe of it. He knew life was a celebration.

Jesus, Ph.D., may take us out of our comfort zone. He sets the perfect example of psychological and spiritual balance. We can't go through life simply thinking, nor can we go through life simply feeling. We must synchronize both into our lives! Then we can be fully alive, and fully human, and not worry whether or not our critics or friends see us sweat!

Questions to Ponder:

1. Are you in touch with your feelings?
2. Are you in touch with the feelings of those around you?
3. Are you strong enough to let your loved ones see your vulnerable places?

Psychological Insight

Allow yourself to feel life and to appreciate its beauty. Remember that compassion and empathy are great companions to your personality. Become psychologically healthy and balanced by getting in touch with your feelings.

"Do not store up for yourselves treasures on earth, where moth and rust destroy, and where thieves break in and steal, but store up for yourselves treasures in heaven."

(Matthew 6:19-20)

He Taught Us Not to Worry

"Never doubt in the dark what God has told you in the light."

A mother of thirteen children was interviewed by a local newspaper reporter. Impressed that the woman had raised the children without the help of a husband, the reporter asked for the secret to her success. The mother replied, "Many years ago, God and I made an agreement that I would do the praying and He would do the worrying."

Sounds like an agreement worth following!

Jesus, Ph.D., knew the negative results of worry. When we worry, we become emotionally and psychologically off-balance. Worry:

· Distracts us from our goals.

· Saps our energy.

· Leads us into depression.

· Steals our happiness.

Jesus' advice to worriers is, "Therefore I tell you, do not worry about your life, what you will eat or what you will drink, or about your body what you will wear. Is not life more than food, and the body more than clothing?[26] ... But if God so clothes the grass of the field, ... will He not much more clothe you?...So do not worry about tomorrow, for tomorrow will bring worries of its own. Today's trouble is enough for today."[27]

God loves you, knows what you need, and will provide for you. Jesus believed this truth, acted on it, and lived by it. He teaches us to do the same. Jesus made a conscious decision not to worry.

When I was forty-nine, I decided to go back to school full-time. Many of my friends thought that I was crazy or courageous—and they weren't sure which! At the same time, my son Matthew came to live with me, which increased my financial obligations. I worried about my ability to cope financially, as well as my ability to go back to school.

One tool that helped me was to replay positive self-talk. I told myself, "Tom, you've done this before and made it. You've done your undergraduate work, and three years of seminary work. You made it then, and you'll make it now! You have crossed your Red Sea more than once."

It also helped to share my anxiety with a close friend. He told me I was gutsy to go back to school, and assured me that it was a wise move no matter what my age was. Then he asked me if I thought God had ever abandoned me in my life. I quickly responded, "Absolutely not." "Then," said my friend, "He won't abandon you now."

I needed to hear those words as I struggled with my decision. They were the right words for the right moment.

Many people are surprised that I view worry as a lack of faith, whether the worrier is a Jew, Hindu, Buddhist, Muslim, or a Christian. In the past, we might have seen worry as only a psychological problem, but it is also a spiritual one.

The anticipated Y2K problem at the turn of the millenium caused endless worry for government officials and business people, as well as the average person. Many of my friends decided not to travel too far from home as December 31, 1999, approached, and others stockpiled food and water. Fortunately, none of these problems materialized. Fear, affects many people.

We seldom worry about the past unless we haven't resolved it or we are trying to hide something. Instead, our worries may center around our own personal needs or the needs of others. We worry about things that will never happen. We worry about things we can't change, or that we have no control over. Codependents are master worriers because they not only worry about their own personal problems, but think it is their responsibility to worry and solve other people's problems. Such worry is a full-time job!

Jane was having a rough session. Tears ran down her face as she sat anxiously wringing her hands. She had been divorced for five years and had received no emotional support or child support from her ex-husband in parenting her ten-year-old son Michael. Her parents had moved away, and her only sister lived in another state. Jane was feeling the pain of abandonment.

Jane doubted her ability as a mother. Her loneliness created a ghetto she seemed unable to get out of. Every night, she tossed and turned because of her worry, and her worry was driving her into poor health.

I asked Jane several questions about her life.

"Jane, despite your worrying, do you and Michael have food on the table?"

She nodded.

"Do you have clothes to wear?"

She said, "Yes."

"Do you have a dependable car to drive?"

"Yes," she said, after some hesitation.

"Are you in good health?"

"Yes," she answered immediately, "very good health."

Jane had a lot to be thankful for. God was already working in her life! My questions were not an attempt to minimize the many concerns she had. Her worry, however, did not increase her good health, her food supply, or the clothes she possessed. In fact, her worry probably decreased what she had, because her focus was on poverty rather than prosperity. The universe never rewards a negative approach or a lack of faith. Rather, the more you expect from the universe, the more it gives! If worry will not add or subtract from what you have, why not give it up? The same amount will be yours without worrying.

When we say "Worry doesn't change anything" we are wrong. Worry changes our health and our state of mind. I believe worry is a prerequisite to cancer and a whole host of diseases. Worry, when it's obsessive, will steal our happiness. It makes us too tired to live peacefully in the present. Worry fills our lives with toxic waste.

Worry has a common denominator. It is a simple lack of faith in ourselves, and especially a lack of faith in God. If you want the peace of mind the Great Psychologist of life desires to give you, stop worrying! [28]

The main problem with worry is that we live with inconsistencies, such as:

· I am a child of God—I am an orphan.

· God will take care of me—if I don't take care of myself, no one will help me.

· God is always with me—I am alone

· If I believe, I will have what I need—what I need I will not have.

· I am loved, have always been loved, and will always be loved—I am unlovable.

Many of us believe the first set of principles, but accept and live by the second set. This gives us a lot to worry about. If I am really an orphan, if I am really alone, if I am not loved, then worry here I come! If we immerse ourselves in the first truths, there will be little room for worry. Sure, we will be concerned about things sometimes. A little anxiety is acceptable in life. But to worry needlessly is foolish.

The next time you start worrying, think about these statements:

· You are the pinnacle of God's creation.

· God is always with us. Always.

· God will supply what we need.

· God has created a world of abundance for you.

· If you believe you can—you can!

· Jesus said, "Ask and it will be given to you."[29]

These are not psychological "feel good" statements. They are eternal truths which, if you accept them and work them into the fabric of your life, will be the greatest deterrents to worry.

Look at these truths as promises from the Great Psychologist. These truths have become powerful tools for your psychological health.

Questions to Ponder:

1. What do you worry about the most right now?
2. How many times during the day do you find yourself worrying?
3. Is your worry a lack of fully believing what God has promised you? Name some ways He is blessing and providing for you at this time.

Psychological Insight

Worry is 99 percent unproductive. Live in the present. Believe God loves you, knows where you are in your life, and will take care of you. Make a commitment to refuse to worry.

He Taught Us to Keep Our Hearts Pure

"The impure heart can never see the world clearly."

Several years ago, I was on an airplane flying to Chicago through gray, dreary, skies. The plane was entombed in banks of thick clouds, and it was obvious the pilot was flying by instruments because we couldn't see a thing. Visibility was zero. For a brief moment, I was frightened. I closed my eyes, and tried to relax.

When I opened my eyes again, the plane had climbed several hundred feet. Suddenly, it broke through the clouds and the plane was bathed in radiant sunshine. The sky was crystal clear. When I looked out the window, it seemed as if I could see forever. Visibility appeared to be unlimited. It was an exhilarating experience.

Some days, nothing seems to be clear in our lives and visibility is at a minimum. We feel as if our minds are in a fog. Other days, our minds are clear, and we feel as if we can see into eternity.

The pure in heart have greater visibility. They see life clearly, and their minds are uncluttered by the distractions that create foggy thinking. Because they are in harmony with God, more is revealed to them.

In the Gospel of John, Philip, a follower of Jesus, goes to get Nathaniel and tell him that he has found the Messiah promised by Moses and the prophets. Philip urges Nathaniel to "Come and see," and Nathaniel does! When Jesus sees Nathaniel coming toward Him, He says,[30] "He is truly an Israelite in whom there is no guile."

The word "guile" Jesus used means a person without bitterness. Jesus was telling His followers that Nathaniel's heart was pure, and not poisoned with bitterness. His mind and his heart were not petty. Nathaniel made the choice to have a pure heart. Would that Jesus would describe you and me this way! What a supreme compliment Jesus gave Nathaniel.

The world needs a lot more Nathaniels!

A pure heart is critical to our psychological well-being, just as a gyroscope is to a ship. When we allow ourselves to be governed by impure thoughts such as jealousy, greed, revenge, envy, and lust, we are contaminating ourselves. These thoughts will obsess us.

A pure heart is also like clear vision. When our vision is blurred, it affects the equilibrium of our entire body. Walking becomes difficult, if not impossible.

In the Sermon on the Mount, Jesus said, [31]"Blessed are the pure in heart, for they will see God." When Jesus talks about the pure in heart, He does not mean one who is sinless as much as one who has a single-mindedness or sincerity. Purity is a passionate aspiration toward holiness.

As Jesus shared His insights with His disciples, He made it clear to them that it is not what is outside of us that makes us pure, it is what is within. Jesus was interested in our thoughts, and wants them to be pure. We accept the saying, "as a man thinks, so he is." If we think angry thoughts, we become angry. If we think greedy thoughts, we become greedy. On the other hand, if we think loving thoughts, we have the greatest possibility to love. As we think, so is our purity of heart either enhanced or diminished.

Some may interpret the words of Jesus to mean that at a future time, the pure in heart will see God face to face. While I believe this is true, His words also mean that one who is pure in heart has the possibility of seeing God in the present. The pure in heart may see God at work today, not only in his life, but in the lives of others. They will behold life now, and though not always obvious, see the hand of God where others are blind to His presence. Only the pure can see the purity and holiness of the living God.

The important question is, how do we become pure in heart? If we are pure in heart, how do we maintain that purity? At a recent seminar, I was asked these questions. In response, I had the individuals imagine a vase filled with marbles up to the top. Then, I asked them to think of the marbles in the vase as good and positive. Then, I had them imagine someone coming along with a new bag of marbles—representing everything that is impure, ugly and evil in the world. They ask you to put them in the vase. You respond, "I can't, the vase is already full." The person persists. You end up putting the new marbles in by taking some of the old marbles out.

Think of your heart and spirit as a glass vase. As long as you keep your heart, or vase, filled with good, positive, thoughts, there is no room for negative things to grow. Your heart is full of goodness. The letter to the Philippeans helps me remember this. "Finally, brethren, whatever is true, whatever is honorable, whatever is just, whatever is pure, whatever is lovely, whatever is gracious, if there is any excellence, if there is anything worthy of praise, think about these things."[32]

The writer is challenging us to focus on the higher things of life. Remember, the principle of focus states that our energy always follows our focus, and that the content of our focus will expand. Imagine what is good, true, righteous, and beautiful in our life expanding. Imagine what can happen when we refuse to let negative thoughts into our minds. Imagine the negative being squeezed out by the good that is mushrooming in abundance. If something doesn't contribute to your peace of mind and well-being, throw it out. Fill your heart to the very top so nothing that is negative can squeeze in. The dividend is purity of heart.

Many people I know have been contaminated by impure thoughts and experiences. Impurity creates a vacuum in our life. This emptiness, or void, attacks our wholeness. We feel as if something is missing in our life. Whatever is closest to the vacuum gets sucked in, and is often unhealthy for our peace of mind and well-being.

Addiction is also a great thief of purity. Addiction feeds on vacuums. It creeps into our lives when we avoid a problem we need to address. Addiction creates a new problem, and the new problem is usually bigger than the original problem.

Andrew knows the power of addiction first-hand. When he came to me for help, he had already failed once to kick his addiction. He was introduced to drugs when he was seventeen by his high school buddies. After graduation, and separation from his friends, he quit using drugs.

Andrew never felt good enough to earn his father's approval. After graduation, Andrew had entered into the family business, a local mechanic repair shop. Andrew hoped working with his father would help bring them together, but they often bumped heads. There were constant stormy confrontations, and they both discovered they had big egos. Though neither admitted it, they were both a lot alike. However, after six months, Andrew quit. He decided to go back to school to study computer programming. Andrew's father berated him, calling him a traitor and claiming he would never amount to anything. Upset, angry, Andrew began using drugs again. Eventually, his money was used up and he dropped out of school. The failure drove him even deeper into drug use.

Three years later, Andrew's father died, and he was grief-stricken. The death of his father left him without closure, in a relationship in which he had struggled to find meaning. Andrew missed the funeral—he was too stoned. When he finally hit the bottom, his brother intervened and convinced Andrew to make an appointment with me.

Andrew started out with a problem: a lack of love and communication with his father. Soon, it escalated to a problem with drugs. Finally, he could no longer communicate effectively with his family. The avoidance of the first problem with his father triggered two new problems. Andrew's problem with addiction may plague him all of his life. What Andrew didn't realize was that his addiction was a way of avoiding his feelings, and burying them deep inside himself. The drugs helped him avoid dealing with his issues.

After many months of hard work, Andrew rehabilitated himself. As he moved toward gaining control of his life, and healing, he was moving toward a purity of mind and heart. This came as he resolved the problems he had in his life. Once these problems no longer preoccupied his mind, or poisoned him, he could cleanse his heart of any angry and bitter feelings toward his father, and especially toward himself.

As Andrew healed, he shared with me his embarrassment about his emotional state. He confided to me that he was crying a lot in private. Andrew considered this to be unmanly. I told Andrew to think of his tears as a cleansing of the impure and unclean things in his life. What was left after the washing out would be pure. His tears were not a sign of weakness, but a sign of the process of healing. His tears would make him a better man.

Many of life's experiences contaminate our purity of heart. When someone whispers gossip in our ear, or shares something negative, it contaminates us. When we are driven by greed or jealousy, it contaminates us. Don't let others walk on your head and heart with their dirty feet!

Negative self-talk is one sure way we poison our hearts and minds. How we talk to ourselves will determine how we perceive things, and eventually it will govern how we feel about the things we see.

I often tell people to use positive self-talk as a way of becoming their own best friends. One client told me she likes talking to herself because she always gets the right answers!

Let's look at Steve. He arrives home about 6 P.M. after a hard day at work, and is surprised to see toys scattered all over the living room floor. Probably the work of his four-year-old, he thinks. As he ventures into the kitchen, he discovers some dirty dishes in the sink, and he becomes angry. He says two negative things to himself: "Why the heck didn't Mary clean up? She's downright lazy!" and then, "I bet she sat around and watched television all day." When Mary arrives on the scene, a negative confrontation follows. Steve acts out his angry feelings.

I asked Steve to take the same incident and do some positive self-talk. Rewind back to Steve, arriving at home. Once again he sees the toys scattered around the living room, and dishes in the sink. Steve says to himself, "Hmm, Mary must of had a hard day. I bet little Stevie was a terror." This is followed by "Maybe Mary isn't feeling well today." Then I suggested Steve could help pick up the toys and remove the visible source of irritation.

When Steve used this positive self-talk, he discovered he wasn't as angry. The initial encounter with Mary was positive, not negative, because he programmed himself differently. He began with, "Gee honey, you must have had a hard day. Let me help you!" followed by, "How can I help?"

Steve, using positive self-talk, took a big step toward keeping his heart pure. When he discovered that positive self-talk worked in one area of his life, he began using it in others. He felt empowered.

Talking to yourself is not a sign that you are crazy. It is a sign that you have discovered a valuable tool that can work for you.

We can tell if something is impure when it shatters our wholeness. We know that something is impure when it interrupts the flow of love in our life; love toward ourselves, others, and especially toward God. If it attacks the harmony in our life, it is impure.

Guard your heart. It is one of the most significant sources of your power. Guard what goes into your heart and your mind. Stand firm against what is negative and toxic. Don't entertain temptation, for you are not strong enough to stand against it. Run, don't walk toward the positive in your life. Run toward God.

Being pure is your responsibility, and your greatest challenge. It is your immediate task, and your ultimate goal.

Questions to Ponder:

1. What thoughts or experiences rob you of the purity in your life?

2. What positive self-talk could you use to help yourself get rid of negative thoughts?

3. What problems do you still need to solve that you have avoided?

Psychological Insight

Purity of our hearts and minds is the core of our psychological well-being. It must be a top priority in our life, for from it will spring all of the good things that will fill up our life. Guard well what goes into your mind and heart. Fill it up with love, so you can see life the way God intends you to.

He Knew How to Transcend the Valleys

"Transcendence means to get rid of the macro lens as we view life and to replace it with a wide angle lens."

They were a young couple in love. The day they said "I do," everything was well-planned, from the beautiful flowers to the delicious wedding cake. The vocalist sang, "Wind Beneath My Wings," one of my favorite songs. As I joined Mark and Joy together as husband and wife, I read to them Paul's words from I Corinthians, "Love is patient and kind."[33]

When it was time for me to say a few personal words, I reminded Mark and Joy how easy it was to love each other on this special day, in such a beautiful setting. It was easy for *everyone* to love each other on a day when there was so much happiness and excitement. "The test, I told them, is to love each other when the going gets tough and there are hard times. The test of your love is the ability to transcend the circumstances you find yourself in. The test is in living real life."

Mark and Joy were young and starry-eyed. While I'm not sure they totally understood my words on their wedding day, I have to believe they soon came down to earth. Hopefully they were able to stay in love with each other in the midst of the harsh realities of life. It's easy to stay positive and be loving when things are going well. The real challenge is to be loving in an unloving world; to be positive in the face of negative circumstances.

Jesus, Ph.D. possessed this skill He transcended the circumstances around Him regardless of what they were. The greatest advantage of this skill is you can act rather than react to what is happening at the moment. You are in control, rather than the environment being in control or another person. When we react rather than act, we are giving our power to someone or something else. We let the other person or the circumstances define our behavior.

I often ask my clients to describe a traumatic situation they have lived through. It might be a divorce, or a dysfunctional family situation, or domestic abuse. Then I ask them, "In the middle of that experience, who did you want to be?" Many individuals under pressure act in a way they are later unhappy about or downright ashamed of.

Recently, I counseled a woman who said she was unhappy with herself for striking her husband with a book during a dispute. Adrian assured me that this was out of character for her, and that her husband had "pushed her buttons." Then she told me she was not abusive.

Adrian was looking for some sympathy from me, so she was surprised by my response. "Yes, you are abusive!" I told her. She argued with me some more, but I stuck to my point. "Is hitting your husband abusive?" I asked. She agreed reluctantly, but brought up her husband's emotional and psychological abuse. I agreed with her, but asked, "Did you hit him?" "Yes," was the reluctant answer.

Of course I was compassionate toward Adrian. Her husband was out of control, and she was paying the price in many different ways. Yet Adrian, like so many of us, was allowing a bad situation to overwhelm her. She was responding to a negative situation with negative behaviors of her own. The truth was, Adrian was becoming just like her husband—the exact opposite of what she wanted!

We must transcend our circumstances. Simple? No. It takes tremendous inner strength. To transcend means we must rise above our immediate circumstances, to think and perhaps "pre-think" what we will do when the going gets tough. To transcend our circumstances, we must act positively instead of negatively. We must stay in control instead of losing control. We must make a decision about who we want to be at critical moments in our lives and then be that person. We must rise above the insignificant, and see the big picture. Transcending our circumstances is a learned pattern of behavior that is very important to our psychological well-being. It is a skill that only the strong of heart acquire.

Sheila was only sixteen, but she had the skill of transcendence. Her mother was very controlling, and nagged Sheila that whatever she did was not good enough. Her mother was also physically abusive. One day, during a heated argument, her mother knocked Sheila down and began choking her. "You will listen to me, because I am your mother!" she told Sheila.

As Sheila gasped for air, she blurted out, "If you were my mother, you wouldn't be choking me!" In that split second, Sheila transcended what was happening to her.

She decided to strike back with her words, and not physical force. At that moment, Sheila defined who and what she wanted to be. Her mother, stunned, stopped choking her and moved away from Sheila. It was the last time Sheila was abused by her mother. Even though their relationship is still not close, they are friendly, though distant.

The supreme example of transcending is found in the person of Jesus, Ph.D. Think of Jesus on the Cross. Imagine the chaos around Him.

Two robbers are hanging on either side of Him. The Roman guards gambled over His remaining earthly possessions. His critics came and ridiculed Him, wagging their heads and saying, [34]"If you are the Son of God, come down from the cross." The chief priests, scribes, and elders mocked Him, saying [35]"He saved others; He cannot save Himself." The soldiers pierced His side to be sure He was dead. He was buried in a borrowed tomb.

Was Jesus angry? Did He give back what He got? The answer is an astounding, overwhelming, NO!

This is what Jesus said in His lowest, loneliest, moment: [36]"My God, my God, why hast Thou forsaken Me?" Then He said, [37]"Father, forgive them; for they know not what they do." How many of us could have uttered these words?

[38]"Truly, I say to you, today you will be with Me in paradise." Jesus gave this promise to the thief who believed in Him.

[39]"I thirst." Jesus had a human need, a need for water.

[40]"Behold, your son." And then, "Behold your mother." These words were spoken first to Mary, His mother, and then to John, His disciple. Jesus was asking John to care for His mother after His death. It is recorded that John was faithful to that request.

[41]"Father, into Your hands I commit My Spirit." He came from the Father, and at the end, would give up His Spirit to the same Father.

[42]"It is finished." Jesus endured and was faithful to His mission to the very last breath.

These are the seven last phrases Jesus spoke from the Cross. Jesus had the ability to transcend the negative circumstances around Him during His most critical hours. We can only stand back and say, "Wow! What a Man! What a Messiah!" He rose above the immediate, the negative, the emotionally-charged words of His enemies. He never forgot who He was, and how He wanted to respond.

This model Jesus gives is for the mature and brave of heart; those of deep faith who have done their inner work. We need to strive to follow His example of transcending circumstances.

Questions to Ponder:

1. How do you define transcendence?
2. What negative circumstances do you have difficulty transcending?
3. Do you know someone who models transcendence? How can you learn from their example?

Psychological Insight

Transcendence is a significant key to psychological health. We must look to Jesus as a model for rising above our negative circumstances, and to see the big picture, rather than the little details. Our faith will help us achieve transcendance.

THE POWER OF ACTION

He Taught Us to Stop Blaming Others

"God gave us parents so we can have someone to blame for our problems!"

The judge in the Indianapolis courtroom listened unemotionally to the rambling defense of the famous boxer accused of raping a young woman. The defendant explained that he had endured a difficult childhood, and that he did not harm the victim. Unimpressed by his rationalization, the judge imposed a six-year sentence. She chastised the boxer for not taking responsibility for his behavior, and its consequences.

Change doesn't take place until we take personal responsibility for our life. Responsibility means we are answerable for our words and our behavior, no matter what our circumstances, position in life, or commitments. Many of the clients I see should wear a sign when they walk into my office emblazoned with the word, "irresponsible." Irresponsibility is at the core of many of their problems.

In the first few chapters of Genesis, we see how quickly Adam and Eve were to blame others and avoid taking responsibility for their aggressive actions toward God. When Adam ate the forbidden fruit, he told God it was Eve's fault for putting the negative idea into his mind in the first place. Eve blamed the serpent for her own downfall.

Until their sin, the Garden of Eden was a beautiful sanctuary for Adam and Eve. However, when Adam refuses to take responsibility for his actions, we find him hiding from God.[43]

Adam and Eve had a son, Cain, who committed the first murder in the Bible. In jealous anger, Cain kills his brother Abel and hides his body. When God confronts Cain, Cain shrugs and replies, "How would I know? Am I my brother's keeper?" The text suggests that God reacted with silence. Why? Because Cain already knew the answer. He chose to avoid blame and responsibility for his actions. Imagine that phrase, "Am I my brother's keeper?"[44] echoing hauntingly throughout the world, over and over again. Imagine the newly-dug dirt, stained with the blood of Cain's brother. "Oh Cain! What have you done?"

Darcee struggled with an addiction problem. In the course of one of her sessions, it came out that Darcee was angry with her father, who had an affair. Her parents' marriage ended in a bitter divorce, and now her father was getting married again—to the woman he had the affair with! Darcee viewed her future mother-in-law as a home-wrecker. Yet Darcee's father blamed her mother for the divorce, saying she didn't pay enough attention to him and his needs. He never apologized for his behavior, or admitted that he was wrong in any way. He chose to avoid responsibility for his actions.

There are four ways we cast blame to the wind.

The first is *rationalization.* Instead of taking responsibility for our actions, we justify them. I hear my clients excuse their behavior, saying, "If she didn't nag me," or "He made me do it," or, "It's her fault."

Another way we avoid responsibility is by *obfuscation,* or taking something that is clear and making it confusing. Perhaps a wife is emotionally cold to her husband. He tries to be warm and tender toward her, but she pushes him away with the comment that the timing is wrong or she is feeling ill. He is confused, although to an outsider, the situation is obvious. She further clouds the issue by complaining that he is needy. "We've been married for five years, and we don't have to keep touching each other."

Other people *minimize* the issue. Michael was having trouble with anger management. When I counseled him in my office, I asked him about a week-long cruise and extra-marital affair that he had. Michael told me he was there to talk about his anger, not his marriage. When I persisted, he said a national survey showed that one out of every three men cheated on their wives, and it was no big deal. "Everybody's doing it," Michael said. He paused at the surprised look on my face. When I asked him if I could repeat that statement to his wife, he became angry and tried to end the session.

The last method we use to avoid responsibility is *denial.* If you've ever confronted an alcoholic, you've probably run up against a wall of denial. When you talk to them about their drinking problems, they are apt to say, "What problem?" Like an ostrich, they stick their heads in the sand.

Jesus Ph.D.

The Great Psychologist encountered several individuals who took responsibility for their lives. We're told that Jesus and Zacchaeus had lunch together, but we're not told about their conversation. We do know that when Jesus and Zacchaeus were finished, Zacchaeus had determined to give half of his riches to the poor, and to repay fourfold anyone he had cheated. He took responsibility for his actions. He paid them back.[45]

The woman caught in adultery never protested. We read in the Book of John that she was caught in the act. Even this, in my own counseling practice, has never stopped anyone from denial! When Jesus asked the woman, "Where are those accusers of yours?" She simply told him they were gone. Jesus said, [46]"Neither do I condemn you."

Another woman touched Jesus' garment, seeking to be healed. Her hopes of touching his garment and then slipping away still anonymous, were dashed when Jesus stopped and said, [47]"Who touched me?" The woman came forward and took ownership of her behavior, and told him candidly why she had behaved as she had.

When the prodigal son came home, it says us he took responsibility for blowing it. "Father, I have sinned against heaven and before you; I am no longer worthy to be called your son."[48] He made no excuses for his behavior.

The two thieves crucified on either side of Jesus are a contrast in behavior. One hurls insults at Jesus, saying, "Aren't you the Christ? Save yourself and us." The other thief recognized that he deserved his punishment and said, [49]"We are punished justly, for we are getting what our deeds deserve. But this man has done nothing wrong." Then he said, "Jesus, remember me when you come into your kingdom." Thrilling words! Jesus answered him, "I tell you the truth, today you will be with me in paradise.[50]

Jesus blesses each of these individuals who took responsibility for their actions. However, there were those who found no comforting words or healing from the Great Psychologist. The Pharisees and other religious leaders of His time came in for His harshest words of criticism and anger. It says Jesus told them, [51]"You travel over land and sea to win a single convert, and . . . make him twice as much a son of hell as you are. ... You tithe down to the last mint leaf in your garden, but ignore the important things—justice, and mercy, and faith." The Pharisees did not take responsibility for their sinful ways. Jesus summarizes His feelings about hypocritical religious leaders in these words, [52]"You are those who justify yourselves in the sight of others; but God knows your hearts."

Julie was always considered the black sheep in her family. When she was sixteen, her father embezzled money from his employer. Both parents blamed Julie, saying, "We were trying to keep you in private school, and buy you a new car." Julie told me tearfully, "I didn't ask them to do any of this for me." She completely accepted her role as the scapegoat for her parents mistakes.

As an adult, her mother constantly told Julie how pretty and successful her older sister was. This decimated Julie's self-esteem. Julie had also recently married an abusive husband, Ryan, who further damaged her self-esteem. When she shared with her mother-in-law that Ryan had hit her several times, her mother-in-law shrugged and said it was no big deal. "In time, Ryan will outgrow it" was her philosophy. Incidentally, Ryan's father, who abused his mother, never did outgrow it.

Today, Julie is on the road to recovery. She's not buying those dysfunctional messages other have given her for so long! She will recover because of her desire and persistence. She is taking responsibility for her own life, and the Great Psychologist is already blessing her.

Jesus calls us to stop making excuses for our behavior. Unless we take complete responsibility for our actions, we will never be spiritually and psychologically healthy and whole. In this way, we move toward peace and healing. Jesus, Ph.D. pushes us to take this step toward growth and positive change.

Questions to Ponder:

1. What do you need to take responsibility for in your life?

2. Who is responsible for the failures in your life? Explain!

3. Is there someone in your life that you need to say you are sorry to, because you have blamed them?

Psychological Insight

We will be psychologically unhealthy as long as we blame others for our problems. Healing in our lives will not begin until we take this step. Blaming others blocks the good things that can happen in our lives. When we take full responsibility for our life, we move toward psychological balance.

He Worked a Program and Taught Us to Do the Same

"People with goals succeed because they map out their destination."

Every effective psychologist has a plan, or program, that they use to help their clients. A plan is a concept or an idea you wish to achieve; a program is a plan in action.

The more specific the program, the more effective it is. This plan may not belong to the therapist, but to the one who seeks healing. In fact, this is the better way to proceed.

Ernie Larsen, an invaluable contributor to the field of addiction and recovery, emphasizes that we all should be working a program. If not, we are missing the boat. I agree with Larson, but I believe that having a plan and program, and working that program may be the most single, important ingredient to success or failure in life. Your program doesn't have to be complex; in fact, the simpler the better. But the bottom line is, you need to have a program.

Jesus, Ph.D. had a plan and a program, and it is obvious that He stuck to it. He planned it from the beginning. In fact, He probably planned it before He got here! He had thirty years before He began His public life, and during those years He came up with a plan, and set His goals.

There was nothing random about Jesus, Ph.D. He was the most significant person in history with the most significant message both spiritually and psychologically. Jesus did not wander around Galilee with some vague idea of what He wanted to do. He made every step count and He made it clear by His words that He was even on a timetable. Jesus was a careful manager of His time and His energy. More than once He stated, "my time has not yet come." He visited the most populated cities and towns talking to as many people as possible. Within His heart and mind there was a blueprint he used to accomplish His mission. He planned what He wanted to say, to whom He wanted to say it, and even how He needed to say it.

It may be helpful to divide a program into three parts:

· The ideas that you have.

· The implementation of these ideas.

· The means by which you will accomplish this plan and bring it to completion.

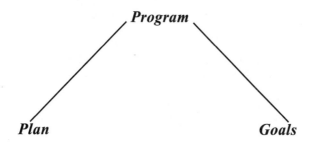

It might sound pretentious to suggest that Jesus had a 12 Step Program, and I don't want to superimpose on Scriptures something that simply was not there. However, if we can concede that He had a plan, a program, and goals that He believed in and consequently was committed to, I think this is what His 12 Step Program might have looked like:

Jesus' 12 Step Program

1.   Accept the belief that the Highest Power in the Universe is God, our Father.

2.   We are helpless to save ourselves from our human predicament without help from God.

3.   Pray to God on a daily basis and remain in constant contact.

4.   Don't judge others. If you must judge, judge yourself and take responsibility for your actions.

5.   Keep the Kingdom of God as your priority, and what you need will be given to you.

6.   Love people, and treat everyone, regardless of race, creed, or status, as a child of God.

7.   Live by your faith and believe all things are possible. They are!

8.   Forgive on a daily basis and remember that is how you are forgiven.

9.   Use your personal gifts wisely and in all things glorify God.

10. Take control of every aspect of your life.

11. Worry is meaningless and unproductive, believe that in every moment of your life God is there and will care for you.

12. Seek truth and wisdom in every word and deed in your life for it leads to eternal life.

This is a program that can change your life. Why not use it and begin to discover the new spiritual and psychological power that can be released in your life?

Remember, the purpose of a plan is to plan your work. The purpose of a program is to work your plan and to maintain the path you have chosen in life. Your program keeps your plan in front of you on a daily basis. Your program is also the bridge between your plan and your work, thus moving you toward your goals. The more vague you are about your plan and your goals, the less likely you are to succeed. Be specific with your program. The more specific you are, the more likely you will get to the other side of your bridge.

Keep in mind that:

- PURPOSE gives meaning to focus
- FOCUS tells you what to concentrate on
- A PLAN is what you decide to do in life
- A PROGRAM is working your plan
- A GOAL is where you want your plan to end up
- The ENERGY to do it all will come from within

Questions to Ponder:

1. What is your plan for your life?

2. What are your ultimate goals you would like to achieve? Be specific.

3. As you look at Jesus' 12 Step Program, which steps are the hardest?

Psychological Insight

Start now with your plan. Have a goal or goals you want to reach and come up with a specific program on how to get there. Once you have done this, work your program on a daily basis. Use Jesus' 12 Step Program as your model and guide.

He Had a Dynamic View of Life

"The earth in which we live is too wonderful for anybody to truly realize. Does any human being ever realize life while they are living it? Perhaps, a few, maybe a saint or a poet."

Thorton Wilder, Our Town, Act 3 (1938)

Perhaps the most tactless thing I did in my professional life occurred when I was a minister. My lawyer friend, John, called me one day, and said he was recommending that a couple who had come to him to file for divorce come and see me instead. He was convinced that they still loved each other, and that their marriage of 20 years could be saved. Would I work with them toward a possible reconciliation?

Our first counseling session was stormy. Clifford and Elizabeth blamed each other for the problems in their marriage, and neither one would accept responsibility. The spark had gone out of their relationship, and intimacy levels were about zero. They seldom talked or ate together, and were sleeping in separate bedrooms.

Clifford loved movies, and was a projectionist at the local movie theater. The fun had gone out of his work, however, and he was bored with his job. When he came home late at night, his wife Elizabeth was often in bed. His days were an endless, dull, routine.

One evening, as Clifford was describing his blah, colorless life, he asked me what I thought. Before I could help myself, I blurted out, "You are the most boring person I have ever met in my life!" No sooner were the words out of my mouth than I thought, "Oh my gosh, did I really say that?"

Clifford's shocked face showed me that I had. Stunned, he asked me to repeat myself.

I was foolish enough to tell him again.

Slowly, Clifford asked me to tell him why I thought he was so boring.

"Cliff, you are not really living! You are vegetating in a routine of work, sleep, eat, day after day after day. You and your wife are living like strangers in the same house! If we put your life on the big screen, you would fall asleep watching your own movie."

I am still amazed that Clifford stayed in the chair and didn't walk out on me. After he left for home, I chastised myself for being a tactless, insensitive, fool. I spent the rest of my evening trying to recover from "hoof and mouth disease."

Clifford went home and told his wife what I had said. Then he told John, his lawyer. Then he told his friends and his family. To his amazement, most of them agreed with my assessment. After thinking about it, he concluded that as harsh as my judgment was, I was absolutely right! At his next visit, Clifford thanked me for my frankness. From that point forward, Clifford changed his life. When I last saw them both, they had mended much of their marriage.

Jesus wants us to live life to the fullest. Many of the Jews who heard Jesus speak believed they already had a full life, and that Jesus had nothing to offer. Who was He to tell them what life was about? After all, they were the favored children of Israel, the descendants of Abraham and Moses. They had the big answers in life, and didn't need to listen to a young upstart. Yet Jesus' words were simple and to the point,[54]" I came that they may have life, and have it more abundantly."

How do you see life? Is it exciting and fascinating, or is it boring and dull? To some, life is just a simple physical journey from point A to point B. This puts the journey of life on a horizontal plane. Along this plane, we find many who are stagnating. I don't call this living. I call it mere existence. The surprise is how many individuals are willing to settle for this kind of life.

There is another kind of life—a pilgrimage rather than a journey. A pilgrimage is an adventure of faith where life is seen as an exciting expression of what we believe. There is nothing boring about a pilgrimage. There will be valleys, there will be mountains, there will be calms and fierce storms, but the rainbows are beautiful.

This pilgrimage is ever-spiraling upward to culminate when we stand before the Wonderful Counselor promised in Isaiah.

Have you ever asked someone how it's going, and they reply, "The same old same old." This answer makes me want to yawn. It puts you to sleep. Part of me wants to retort, "It's your fault that it is the same old same old." Then I want to scream, "So what are you going to do about it?"

If you are living the "same old same old," you need to get out of your rut. A rut is just a coffin without the sides up yet. If you see someone coming toward you with a hammer and nails, you better start climbing out—quick!

I call Jesus' approach to life the "light-switch principle." Picture the life you are living in as a room that you enter into on a daily basis. You know this room intimately; you have been there since birth. It is your comfort zone. Along comes Jesus, and suggests that you flip on the light switch, which you do. Wow! You thought you knew this room before, but now you realize there are many details you missed. Amazing!

Now, think of your faith as the light switch. When you see life through the lens of faith—turn on the light—it will change your attitude, your behavior, and your world immediately.

Jesus wants us to live a life led by the Spirit.[55] He said, "The wind blows where it chooses, and you will hear the sound of it, but you do not know where it comes from or where it goes. So it is with everyone born of the Spirit."

If our life is simply of the flesh; a physical, earthly, journey of eating, drinking, and grabbing everything in life you can, it is a life of stagnation and death. If, however, you move toward the life led and reborn by the Spirit— God's Spirit—then life is a pilgrimage. Spirit and faith will completely change the way you perceive life, how you experience it, and how you live it.

No wonder Jesus believes in a dynamic life! He knows the mystery of life and the depths and height our lives can reach. He experienced its sacredness and beauty. He endured pain and suffering. He rejoiced, He laughed, He had compassion, and He wept at the loss of a friend. He felt the sting of betrayal. He knew life was more than just our daily bread. He looked beyond the precious present to capture a glimpse of eternity, which He claims begins *now*. He knew death first-hand, and walked out of a grave alive.

"Come," says Jesus, "Turn on the light in your life, and accept the kingdom of rebirth that embraces the present with the dynamic touch of eternity."

Questions to Ponder:

1. How do you view life? Describe.
2. Do you find life basically boring, just okay, or exciting?
3. How do you want your life to change in the next year? In the next five years?

Psychological Insight

Life is an exciting, creative force. When life is led by the Spirit instead of the flesh, it changes from a journey to a pilgrimage. Life should be measured by our experiences and meaningful encounters with God, not by time or events. When we allow this to occur, our lives will be transformed from tedious to fullness.

He Used His Gifts Wisely

"Only the wise know our gifts are lent to be spent."

Several years ago I met an artist whose artwork I had always admired. After I told him how much I appreciated his work, he told me a little bit about his life.

One day, as the artist traveled to his home from an art fair, he was caught in a terrible storm. A voice penetrated the thunder from the storm and said, "What are you doing for Me?" He looked around. He was alone.

Again he heard the voice. "What are you doing for me?" This time, the artist felt compelled to reply, "I am painting ships and earning a living for my family."

"Yes, I know," the voice continued, "but what are you doing for Me?"

Unnerved, the artist fell silent. When he arrived home, he felt driven to paint. Working furiously, he painted all night until he fell asleep, exhausted. When he awoke the next morning, he looked in surprise at his painting. Dark clouds filled the canvas, and in the center was Jesus, crucified in agony on the Cross. Behind the clouds were two piercing, penetrating, eyes.

Wherever he went in his studio, he felt the eyes focused on him. He was haunted by the question, "What are you doing for Me?" The artist reviewed his life, and realized that in all of his work he had never thought about serving God with his gifts. Finally, he came to the admission that his work was all for himself—none of it was for God. From that day on, the themes of his work changed as well as his attitude. He painted to the glory of God.

All of us are given unique gifts and talents. Sometimes they are obvious, sometimes they are hidden and obscure. Great or small, the gifts we have are blessings from God. We must decide what gifts we have been granted, and how we will use them to His glory.

The first major challenge Jesus faced as He began His public life was deciding how to use His gifts. He was 30 years old, and the Gospel of Matthew tells us, [56]"Then Jesus was led up by the Spirit into the wilderness to be tempted by the devil." Forty days later, Jesus was coming off of a fast and He was famished! Satan tempted Him in three ways:

1. He was hungry, and Satan told Him to turn the stones into bread.

2. Satan told Jesus to throw Himself off of a high place, and He would be rescued by angels, and receive public recognition.

3. Satan invited Jesus to worship Him, and He would give kingdoms to Jesus.

Satan knew that Jesus had unlimited, divine, power at His fingertips that He could use. He encouraged Jesus to use His power selfishly to satisfy Himself: turning stones into food, receiving public recognition, and the accumulation of riches and wealth as a reward for worshiping the tempter. The temptations of food, popularity, and wealth fit right into our 21st Century. But at the center of all three temptations is the question, "My Father has given me gifts, do I use them to glorify Him or do I use them for myself?"

It was obvious as I counseled my client, George, that he was angry with everyone: his father, his mother, his brother, his wife. He was angry about his past. He was angry about his current circumstances. He was angry about being in my office, especially since he was there because of a court order from a judge who told him to work on his anger.

George was tremendously successful financially. He proudly shared with me that he was a self-made man and now a multi-millionaire. While he tried not to boast about his money, it always came up, along with his belief that I was over-charging him. He berated me about this even though he was paying only 60 percent of my rate.

After one session, I asked him a simple question that seemed to stump him, "George, what are you giving back?" He seemed confused by my question, so I continued, "If you believe God has given all this to you, what are you giving back?" George had no answer.

It's easy to be critical of George, but how would you answer that question? Unfortunately, sometimes our attempts to give back are too cheap. Yes, cheap! Ralph Waldo Emerson once said that "our gift cannot be an excuse for not giving ourselves." We have all been guilty of this at one time or another. A coin in the coffer instead of giving our time. Some money for our children instead of spending time with them. We can't fool them! Many an adult son or daughter has sat in my office and declared, "I wish my mother or father worked less and I had more time with them." While the parents were working for bigger houses and more possessions for their kids, the gift the children wanted was their parents.

John Milton, the English poet, was well acquainted with hardships and obstacles. His wife, Mary, died three days after giving birth to their son, who also died shortly after. At the same time, Milton began losing his vision and was soon totally blind. His locked up his grief inside of himself; his pen was silent.

Then in 1352, he broke the drought that had dried up his heart and wrote these words in a poem:

On His Blindness

When I consider how my light is spent,
E're half my days in this dark world and wide
And that one Talent which is death to hide
Lodg'd with me useless, though my Soul more
bent to serve therewith my Maker, and present
My true account, least he returning chide,

Doth God exact labour, light deny'd
I fondly ask, but patience to prevent
That murmur, soon replies, God doth not need
Either man's work or his own gifts, who best
Bear his mild yoak, they serve him best, his State
Is Kingly, Thousands at his bidding speed
And post o're land and Ocean without rest:
They also serve who only stand and wait.

Out of these moments of darkness, which found Milton only "standing and waiting," Milton went on to write his greatest work, "Paradise Lost," an epic narrative about the creation and fall of man. It became a classic.

The task before you is to discover your gift. Don't look for the spectacular. Your gift may be something as simple as a cheerful attitude, a smile, or baking an apple pie. If you have difficulty seeing your gifts clearly, ask those who know you well to help you identify them. But to use them wisely is up to you.

What have you given back to Him who is the source of your gifts? Have you given the gift of yourself to those who love you?

Questions to Ponder:

1. What gifts do you believe that you have? If you do not know, ask others to objectively help you with that discovery.

2. How would you rate yourself in the wise use of your gifts?

3. Do you recognize time as a gift to be used?

Psychological Insight

Discover your gifts and use them for others and for the glory of God. This is your way of saying "thank you" to the Giver of the gifts. By the unselfish use of your gifts, you will find fulfillment and joy. Don't forget to give others the gift of yourself!

He Taught Us to Manage Our Anger

"Anger is only one letter away from danger."

Imagine yourself sitting in the office waiting for your first counseling appointment. You've been struggling with a problem with your temper, and you hope your psychologist can help you control your anger.

While you're leafing through some magazines, you spot an unusual picture on the wall. It appears to be a picture of your psychologist, and it appears as if he is in church or synagogue. This isn't a standard photo portrait! Your psychologist appears to be overturning several tables, and in his hand he has a rope that he is using as a whip. The look of anger on his face is obvious and several people are running away in fear from his wrath. At his feet there are animals escaping out of some broken cages. It is a chaotic scene.

You ask the receptionist if this is the psychologist in the picture, and she replies, "Yes, indeed." Puzzled, you wonder, "Am I in the right place?"

When Jesus went to pray in the Temple, He was outraged when he saw the moneychangers and merchants selling doves and animals for sacrifice. He overturned their tables, dumping coins on the ground. Making a whip out of rope, He drove them out.   Jesus said, [57]"It is written, 'My house shall be called a house of prayer'; but you are making it a den of robbers." On the surface, it looks like Jesus overreacted, but when we look more deeply, we see He was angry that the Pharisees and leaders of the Temple had a racket going. They knew that to worship in the Jewish tradition, one needed to offer a sacrifice according to their financial means. However, any offering that was purchased outside of the Temple was usually rejected and turned away. The authorities would point the worshipers to their own merchants, forcing the worshiper to buy at inflated prices. Jesus knew that this was not about worship. It was about money, greed, and profit. He was angry! His house and the house of His Father, was being robbed of its sacredness.

The Great Psychologist was consistent about what angered Him. He was angry with those who were leaders of the people and constantly lead them in the wrong direction. He had scalding words for such leaders. To those who have much light given to them, much light is required. He was angry with hypocrites and those who paraded themselves as religious whose hearts were far from God. Their acts only inflated their own egos and reputations. They were legalistic but had lost the true spirit of believing in God.

Jesus had a right to be angry! The leaders were dealing with other people's lives, and they were not faithful to their calling. They were caught up in their own selfishness, egotism. and pride. They had put themselves before the kingdom of God. Jesus reveals to us that there is such a thing as divine anger; and Jesus, as the Son of God, felt personally violated by their words and deeds.

Jesus talked a lot about being angry with our brothers and sisters. In His own words He declared, [58]"But I say to you that if you are angry with a brother or sister, you will be liable to judgment; and if you insult a brother or sister, you will be liable to the council." There is a footnote that says 'without cause.' The Great Psychologist continues by saying that if you are worshiping in the Temple and you are angry or at odds with your brother, leave your offering at once and go and reconcile with your brother.

Jesus also recounts the story of the prodigal son, who leaves home for the big city and a more exciting life. After he blows his inheritance, the boy comes to his senses and returns home. His joyful father welcomes him back and throws a feast for him. But his older brother hangs back and refuses to join the party. He is upset and angry. The older son was unjustly angry with the younger.

We live in an angry society. The media is filled with stories of angry people abusing each other at home, road rage on the highways, and shootings at work and at school. Marriages end in bitter divorces, with custody battles over the children. Look at these situations that produce anger:

· A divorced mother moves 200 miles away from her child's father, hoping to limit his visitation.

· A father purposely offers his sixteen-year-old daughter a new car as a reward for living with him instead of her mother.

· A mother begins a campaign with the children during visitation to smear their father and to poison the children against him.

· A father abandons his children financially and disappears.

· A mother, still angry about the divorce, continually blocks visitation with the father.

· A divorced parent puts his new family before his first family.

· A twenty-year-old daughter who was molested by her father, confronts him, and he denies it. She also finds out that her mother knew what was going on and chose not to intervene.

I could fill a whole chapter with examples of angry people, especially in the area of children and divorce who have become pawns for our selfish battles in and out of the courtroom. Winning has become more important than what is fair or just. It is in this arena that we have failed the most. It is in this arena that we so desperately need to ask what would Jesus do, and do it.

In our society, there is a new phenomenon that I term "dangling anger." When I use this term, I am describing an anger that is not easily resolved. This anger is often left dangling, for weeks, months, years, for a lifetime. It is important that this anger be resolved.

As I counsel individuals in difficult situations, I know that they are often in anguish. They are angry, and need to release their anger in a constructive way. The good news is that we can break the grip that anger has on our lives. Anger is a decision. Consequently, we must take responsibility for our decision to be angry. We can also decide not to be driven by our anger. Sound simplistic? Maybe. But this is an important starting point.

Your first choice could be to wake up every morning saying, "I refuse to get angry today." Then take the initiative to work out whatever anger there is between you and any other person. Don't let your ego or pride hold you back, just do it. If you don't get things worked out, you have done your part. If you need to vent your anger to a friend, or to a therapist, do that as well. You may have to do this more than once, and then let it go and move on. Your anger is not hurting the other person, it is hurting you.

Pray about the person making you angry. Yes, you read it right! If you say you cannot do this, then you know that you have not forgiven them yet. When you can pray for them, you are moving in the right direction, one of healing and letting go. Do this even if you can't pray it honestly. Continue to do so! It will get easier.

However, if you are still having difficulty letting it go, move on to some other steps. Move away, physically if possible, certainly mentally, from the source of your anger. If it is a situation or a person, distance yourself. Refuse to let your mind continue to be filled with your angry thoughts about the person or the situation. Refuse! Remember you control your thoughts, no one else. How do you do this? You focus on what is good, wholesome, and uplifting to you. Surround yourself with positive situations and people who are supportive to you. You are building a positive support system around you, and the broader that system, the more support, the easier it is to move from negative thoughts to the positive.

Jesus voiced and displayed His anger, but then He always moved on to the good news of His kingdom, and focused on His kingdom. His heart was so filled with love and truth, anger could not gain a permanent foothold in His life to poison Him.

Let it be so with us!

Questions to Ponder:

1. What angers you most in your life?

2. What did your parents teach you about anger?

3. If you have a temper, what are you doing to manage it?

Psychological Insight

Anger under normal circumstances is a sign that we have been violated. It is okay to become angry, but what you do whith your angry is the key to psychological balance. If you direct your anger inward it could lead to depression. Yet, controlling your anger and not lashing out at others is important. Learn how to take time-outs, and not to be driven by your anger. Don't let the sun go down on your anger. Work things out. Only by releasing your anger can you be released as well.

He Retreated Before
He Charged

"If you charge out into the world without knowing what you are going to do when you get there, then you have set yourself up for failure."

How do you face life? Do you prepare for life or do you just let it happen to you? Jesus gives us some excellent examples on what to do as we face our challenges.

Paul urges us to prepare for life by taking up the helmet of salvation and the sword of the Spirit, which is the Word of God. David prepared for his battle with Goliath by asking the God of Israel to bless him. Then he reminded himself of the battles God had already helped him win. King Saul wanted him to prepare by wearing his armor, but David soon found it to be too large for his young body. Perhaps he learned that you can not go to battle in someone's armor, you need to take your own! The rest is history. Solomon prepared for his kingship over Israel by praying for wisdom.

Too bad General Custer didn't prepare before he charged into the Battle of Little Big Horn. Perhaps, he would avoided one of histories worst defeats.

Jesus always retreated before He charged into the battles of life. Before He began the challenges of His ministry, He went into the desert and fasted for forty days, preparing for the difficult days ahead.

Look around you, and you will quickly discover those running out into life unprepared. Once they get out there they have nothing to say. When they do speak, they make fools of themselves. This is why there are so many people that fail.

Jesus prepared in several ways before He "charged" into His tasks:

· He used quiet time

· He prayed

· He affirmed once again who He was

· He renewed His faith

· He rested

· He recreated

· He was in contact with His Highest Power

· He renewed His mission.

By retreating before He charged, He had the best opportunity for positive results. No wonder He stayed in control!

Questions to Ponder:

1. How do you prepare to face the giants in your life?

2. Have you set aside some quiet time to retreat before you charge?

3. Think of a circumstance when you let life happen to you without adequate preparation. How could you handle this situation differently in the future?

Psychological Insight

It is important to retreat and prepare for the tasks that confront you in your life. By preparing and using the tools that God has provided for you, you are assured of your greatest success. The Great Psychologist promises to go with you to face your Goliath.

He Took Control of His Life

*"The man who masters
his own soul will forever
be called conqueror of conquerors."*
—Planutus

Victor Frankl, a Jewish psychiatrist imprisoned in a concentration camp during World War II, was stripped naked by his German captors and left with only his gold wedding ring on his finger. He feared they were taking him to the gas chamber. His wedding ring was his last earthly possession, and represented the precious memory of his love for his wife and children who had been torn away from him. A guard, spotting the ring, demanded to have it and threatened Frankl with his life if he didn't take it off.

In that moment, Frankl realizes that he cannot control his circumstances. He cannot hang on to any earthly possessions. The only thing left in his control is his attitude and his spirit. He can only control how he will perceive and react to what is happening to him. They could capture his body, but not his spirit. It was this truth that helped Frankl survive Auschwitz.

People who are not in control of their life usually suffer from the "unholy trinity"—depression, low self-esteem, and a victim mentality.

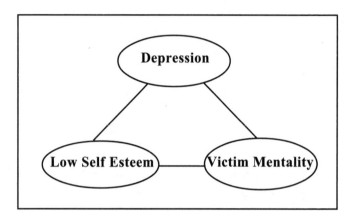

Each of these problem areas feed off of each other. When a person loses control of their life and feels like a victim, their state of mind will usually lead to depression. Whether low self-esteem is the result of being a victim, or the cause of it, is not always clear, but both are part of the same equation.

This "unholy trinity" is more than just words on a page. For many, the loss of control in their life, and the resulting depression, low self-esteem, and victim mentality, means deep despair.

One of the quickest ways to give away your power is to be a reactionary, taking your cues from the environment around you. I counseled a man who came in for domestic abuse counseling who modeled this behavior. Roger was a handsome, successful, executive in his mid-thirties. After several sessions, I asked him, "What would you do if someone came up and hit you?" Without hesitation, he said, "I'd hit them back!" I asked him the same question again, and asked for a different answer. Again he said, "I'd hit them back!" After he answered me this way a third time, I was frustrated. But Roger stood firm, saying, "If someone hits you, there are no other options. You hit them back."

Roger had spent his whole life hitting back. He was reactionary. He couldn't see how reacting to events allowed others to set him up and control his actions. No wonder he was in trouble with the law and the court system!

We lose control in our life when we let others make decisions that should have been ours alone to make, or are indecisive. There's a story about a man who was fishing upriver from Niagara Falls, and kept putting off the decision to take his boat back to the shore. Soon he found himself caught in the current of the river, with the sound of the thundering falls getting louder and louder. Fortunately, a helicopter was dispatched to rescue him.

We must stay in control of our own lives, yet not succumb to the temptation to selfishly control the lives of others. The desire for power and selfish control is at the heart of the wave of domestic abuse that is sweeping over our country. Statistics say that 95 percent of the abusers in our society are men. However, this does not excuse the growing number of aggressive and abusive women.

When I tell a couple to give up control in a relationship, they are usually shocked, thinking it will make their relationship worse. The abusive person may be trying to stop their significant other or spouse from talking to friends, limiting time going out, informing the other person with whom he or she can talk, or what to watch on television. All such attempts have nothing to do with love. At the core of this control issue is an attempt to play God by assuming the abusive person knows what is best for the other person. This control leads to destructive patterns of behavior, and injures others, emotionally, psychologically, and physically. These control patterns usually escalate to an intense, dangerous level unless there is an intervention. We don't need to control other people. Our responsibility is only to control ourselves.

We need to take control of our lives—our emotions, our feelings, our thoughts, our finances, and especially our behavior. All other areas are off-limits. If we are aggressively taking control of our lives in these areas, we will be so busy we won't have time to control anyone else's life! We'll have our hands full with our own.

Codependents are notorious for trying to control other's lives—usually while their own life is out of control! They believe if they control the other person's actions that the person will have a happier life and be successful. So they focus on the other person, making their decisions for them, guiding them, and giving them unsolicited advice. The more they focus on someone else, the more they ignore their own life and fail to take care of themselves. They mean well, but their efforts are based on the erroneous premise that they know what is good for someone's life, with dysfunctional results.

Jesus refused to get caught up in negative patterns of abusive behavior. In John 10:18 He says of His power and control as related to His life, "No one takes it from Me, but I lay it down of My own accord. I have power to lay it down, and I have power to take it up again." He was in control of His life.

On one occasion, the chief priests, the elders, and the scribes came to Him while He was teaching in the Temple and asked, "Tell us, by what authority are you doing these things?" Jesus was aware of their motives, and their attempt to entrap Him. He answered, "I will also ask you a question, and you tell me: Did the baptism of John come from heaven, or was it from human origin?" They discussed it with one another, saying, "If we say, 'From heaven,' He will say, 'Why did you not believe him?' But if we say, 'Of human origin,' all the people will stone us; for they are convinced that John was a prophet.'"

Finally, they told Jesus they didn't know the answer. Jesus said to them, "Neither will I tell you what authority I am doing these things."[60]

Jesus was in control of His life, and never gave up His power to another. There were many attempts to control Jesus, but they all failed. He knew He and His Father were one in Spirit and purpose.

When Jesus was tried by Pilate, He remained silent throughout His questioning. To Pilate, it must have appeared that Jesus was a victim of circumstances beyond His control, but surprisingly Jesus didn't look or act like a victim at all. Pilate expected Jesus to plead for His life. Yet Jesus stood confidently silent. I picture Him with a firm, determined look on His face, as if to say, "Have no doubt that I will make it through this. Have no doubt that I am in control." Pilate, unnerved by Jesus' lack of cooperation, finally said, "Do you refuse to speak to me? Do you not know that I have power to release You, and power to crucify You?" [61]

It was then Jesus spoke, and set the record straight. He answers Pilate, "You would have no power over Me unless it had been given you from above."

When Jesus was arrested in the Garden, those who came with their weapons to take Him away were feeling very much in control. However Jesus said, [63]"Do you think that I cannot appeal to My Father, and He will at once send Me more than twelve legions of angels?" Twelve legions of angels would be 72,000! All Jesus had to do was ask, and it would have happened in the blink of an eye.

Jesus did not go to the Cross kicking and whimpering. He did not ask, "Why me?" because He knew. He pressed on with a "just do it" attitude. I believe He laid His own hands down on the Cross in preparation for the nails they would drive through them. Never was a man in more control of His emotions, His feelings, His thoughts, and His actions. He died the same way He lived. Such control under extreme circumstances is incomprehensible to us, and beyond human words to express.

Jesus took control of His life. He invites you to do the same! Are you strong enough to do it?

Questions to Ponder:

1. What do you need to do to take control of your life?

2. Name those areas and be specific about what you plan to do to take control of them?

3. Do others accuse you of being controlling?

Psychological Insight

Strive to be in total control of every aspect of your life: your emotions, your finances, and your behavior. Taking control of your own life will help you to act in positive ways instead of reacting to situations, thus giving your power away. By this you will gain the freedom to rise to your greatest potential.

He Believed That We Can Change Our Lives

"Every saint has a past, and every sinner a future."
—*Oscar Wilde*

Like a phantom, he comes to Jesus under the cover of darkness. Nicodemus is an important religious and political leader, and one of the seventy elders of the Sanhedrin, the supreme court of the Jews. He wanted to talk with Jesus, but it is too risky for his reputation to be seen with Him in the daytime. Despite his fears, Nicodemus believes Jesus to be a prophet from God, capable of miracles.

However good Nicodemus is Jesus tells him he needs to do more if he wants to be a part of God's kingdom. Jesus continues, "I say to you unless one is born anew he cannot see the kingdom of God." Nicodemus is surprised by this revelation and asks, "How can this be?" Nicodemus takes what Jesus said in a literal, physical, way. He adds, "Surely he cannot enter into his mother's womb a second time and be born." (John 3:4). It was not the flesh Jesus had in mind but a more radical and fundamental change. Jesus explained to him that the first birth is of the flesh. The second birth is of the Spirit. The first birth is natural, the second birth is supernatural.[64]

Jesus believes in Nicodemus' ability to change, and expects him to do it! Jesus also knows the problem of a man who wants to be changed and who cannot change himself. Just as therapy is often an intervention into someone's life to bring an insight or a moment of truth, so Jesus is saying the Spirit will intervene in our lives to help bring change at the very center of our beings so we can enter into the life of God.

A man who had once been an uncontrollable alcoholic became a Christian. His fellow workers would often mock him and say, "Surely you don't believe in miracles and things like that. Surely, you can't possibly believe that Jesus turned water into wine." The man was usually stumped by these challenges, but one day God gave him an answer for them, "I don't know whether He turned water into wine when He walked upon this earth, but, one thing I do know, in my own house He has turned beer into furniture!"

Jesus was talking about a life led by the Spirit. Listen to how mysterious this new life is. [65]"The wind blows where it chooses, and you will hear the sound of it, but you do not know where it comes from or where it goes. So it is with everyone born of the Spirit." The word "wind" and the word "spirit" are the same in the Greek.

If our life remains unborn, then it is simply of the flesh, a physical, earthly existence of eat, drink and get all you can. If, as Jesus invited, it is a life led and reborn by the Spirit, His Spirit, then it becomes a pilgrimage. The trip is no longer one of simple reason and rationale, it is that plus faith. These new ingredients, Spirit and faith, will change how you perceive life, how you experience it, what you seek out of it, and consequently, how you live it. Jesus invites all of us to undergo the ultimate change of *re-creation.*

Can people really change their lives? How much can they change their lives? Can we change a little or a lot? These are pertinent questions in a changing world. The key to changing one's life is first to have an earnest desire to do so. I'm not talking about a whim, or a temporary burst of energy, but a deep determination to want change.

Jesus believes you can change your life. His message for us today is, "You can change for good, and continue to grow." Since 1900, the world has grown more than any other time in history. We have also accomplished more and accumulated more information than in all previous centuries. Life has changed drastically even in my own lifetime. Imagine what it is like for Henry, who is ninety-eight years old. He began his life before we had cars, airplanes, telephones, and even television. Think of what he has witnessed.

Information means truth. Truth means freedom, and freedom means growth. Jesus declared, "The truth shall set you free." (John 8:32)

Our learning curve has changed. It was once accepted that we learned most of our information in our early years of our life and then went on into our professions or occupations. We said phrases like, "you can't teach an old dog new tricks," and quite frankly we believed them. We also believed that once you received your education it was over. Then you sat back and used it for the rest of your life. Now there is so much information out there that if you are not in continuing education you are quickly becoming a dinosaur. Would you feel comfortable with a doctor who is fifty-two years old and has never been to a seminar or taken a course since his graduation from medical school in 1968?

Change and growth are more important in our lives than ever before, and if we are not open to it, the world will surely pass us by. Growing is a process, one which never stops. We never say, "That's it, I have grown enough." We should be constantly changing and growing. We'll only stop growing when they lower us into the ground.

People who come to me for counseling often say they want change. Yet they resist it. We are creatures of habit, and the habits are comfortable. Change is different and difficult, and it seldom occurs without getting out of our comfort zone.

Pain is a great catalyst for change. Often, when there is no incentive to change, no change occurs. Pain is a signal within us that something is wrong, something is not in harmony, something needs healing. Sometimes we get used to the pain in our lives and ignore it. Then, instead of it motivating us to change, we end up living with the pain and we raise our threshold of tolerance. The pain no longer drives us to change or to investigate why do we have this pain. We need to listen to our pain, and let it push us to find out what is not in harmony. Then we can make the necessary changes to get our life back to a wholeness. This pain may put us in the valleys of our life where we shed tears, but this pain can also push us to the mountain top. The valley and the mountain top are both necessary experiences of life.

As David sat across from me in my office, I could tell that he was anxious. He leaned forward, and said, "Tom, you know that in three weeks I will not be on a tether anymore." David had been on a tether for more than a year because of his domestic abuse and his drinking problem. His question was, "How can I leave my addiction behind me?" For David, I knew that was the ultimate question. This was his second time he had gotten in trouble for the same problems.

I shared with David that he needed to change. He had to stay out of bars, and away from where there was drinking. Then, I told him he needed new friends; friends who didn't drink and who would be supportive of his new life style. I encouraged him to be a better parent, and do more things with his son.

The key for David was to change his thinking about drinking. Drinking was the enemy for David. You don't compromise with the enemy! He had to stay away from anything that would tempt him into slipping back into old habits. David realized he had to be recovering every single day of his life. He needed to change, if he was to win!

The apostle Paul knew about this change when he declared, [66]"Do not be conformed to this world, but be transformed by the renewing of your minds." The word "transform" means to change, or convert. To be transformed is a daily process. How easy it is to conform to the world! There is a strong pressure to fall into line, to go with the flow, to fit into a cookie-cutter pattern. We feel uneasy about being different. Yet, to be transformed by the renewing of your mind is to hear a different drummer within you and marching to it. This march is uniquely yours.

If you choose to do so, you can undergo the greatest change of your existence. The secret to psychological happiness is the openness to growth and to change. This growth is not a horizontal line; rather, it spirals up toward the Author of change.

Questions to Ponder:

1. What do you still need to change in your life?
2. Can you pinpoint a time in your life when you made several changes? What was the result?
3. Are you open to let the Great Psychologist and His Spirit change and transform you?

Psychological Insight

Change is necessary for growth. The Great Psychologist invites us to change and knows that we have the ability to change if we will open ourselves to use the tools that He provides for us. To change is life, to resist is death.

He Taught Us to Stop Searching for Happiness

"Real happiness is cheap enough, yet how dearly we pay for its counterfeit."
—Hosea Ballou

Everyone wants to be happy. Recently, the author of a book urged making the pursuit of happiness a diligent endeavor. But I believe the search for happiness is one of the most misunderstood ventures of life.

Many people who come to see me professionally believe that therapy will make them happy. Obviously, this is a high expectation, and probably an unrealistic one. Therapy may temporarily make a person miserable and unhappy as they face their problems.

There is no panacea for happiness, no miracle cures. There are no wonder drugs, no magic pills. Happiness doesn't come that easily.

Many people believe that the more money you have, the happier you will be. If this was true, the further we move away from the physical ghettos of our society toward the wealthier communities, the greater our happiness. Yet, some of the most tragic things in our society happen in rich suburban areas, as the Columbine school shootings illustrated. Happiness is no respecter of bank accounts. *People* magazine once followed the lives of lottery winners, and found that several years after winning, many of the winners concluded they were happier before they won the money. Many were amazed at the demands and greed of their family and friends.

The first unhappiness recorded in history began in the most unlikely place—paradise! Adam lived in the most beautiful garden in the world. God handpicked the perfect woman to live as his wife, and Adam was given dominion over all of creation. They had all the food and everything needed for good living. What else could two human beings possibly want?

But Adam and Eve wanted something that was never intended to be theirs. They desired to be like God. The Bible tells us they were driven out of the garden and, soon after, the first murder took place. Suddenly, paradise wasn't paradise anymore.

The Great Psychologist did not promise us happiness. In fact, if you follow his precepts, unhappiness and suffering may follow here on earth. He did say to his disciples that the man who follows His teachings will be blessed, or happy. Yet, Jesus didn't seem to be searching for happiness here on earth.

When happiness is our primary pursuit, we will seldom find it. If you want to be happy, stop searching for happiness. Instead, follow Jesus' model. Jesus searched for ways to serve others. Instead of asking, "What's in it for me?" ask, "How can I make the world a better place?" Rather than saying, "Give me more!" say "How can I make a difference?"

A lot has changed since President John Kennedy epitomized service by saying, "Ask not what your country can do for you, but what you can do for your country." No wonder that was the era of the Peace Corps and similar programs.

Look at our world today. When I interned in an elementary school in a rich suburban area of metropolitan Detroit, a teacher told me that she had fourth graders who left their homes at seven or eight in the morning and didn't see their parents until seven or eight at night. The parents were working hard, trying to support their lifestyle. In today's culture, we are too worried about where we live, what cars we drive, how much money we make, and how well dressed we are.

Happiness comes when we let the significant things in life be our priority. Imagine Jesus. He asked the questions "How can I help you? What can I do for you? What can I give to you?" He didn't ask lightly; he asked with absolute seriousness. Not "Give it to me," but "What can I give?"

Jesus gave everywhere He went, and the blind saw, the lame walked, the lepers were made whole. The sorrowful stopped crying, the depressed were given joy, the lost were found, and the dead were alive again.

The Great Psychologist moved in our world with grace and compassion, going where He was welcome and needed.

Jesus humbled himself and washed the feet of his disciples, then asked them, [67]"Do you know what I have done for you?"

He was their teacher, yet He became their servant.

He is the Messiah, yet he became their servant.

He is the Son of God, yet He became their servant.

Then He challenged the disciples to become servants as well. When there was an outbreak of egotism among the disciples, and they asked Jesus, [68]"Who will be the greatest in the kingdom?" the Great Psychologist made it clear that only through service could anyone hope to be the greatest. In a recent television special about Joan of Arc, she says to the Lady of Burgundy, "I would die if I could not serve others."

Two other things contribute to our happiness. The first is the ability to make personal relationships work. Many individuals are successful in the business world but struggle with their personal relationships. This is true especially of men.

Kenneth had climbed the corporate ladder of success with Ford Motor Company. He made over $250,000 per year, and had a lot of respect from his coworkers. However, at home he had difficulty being a good husband and adequate father to his teenage son and daughter. His own father had been very critical, and his mother's life revolved around his father. His parents had never been supportive of him.

To deal with the stress of his demands at work and the feeling of failure at home, Kenneth began drinking. Ken was successful financially, but a failure in his personal relationships.

Let's break up Ken's life into two categories.

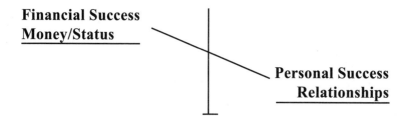

Financial Success
Money/Status

Personal Success
Relationships

As you can see like so many individuals in our society one area is so out of balance with the other.

Sometimes people are workaholics because they don't know how to make relationships work. Kenneth and his wife went through therapy for a year, but then reached a stalemate. After that, their relationship deteriorated back into the old habits. My heart is sad for them. I wish this was an isolated case!

Without happiness in the intimate relationships of life, happiness will probably elude you. Make relationships your primary priority. Frankly, it would better to be successful in your personal life and less successful in your business. It is the wise person who clearly understands that he must put both successes together, and work hard at both.

The most significant relationship you have is with Jesus, the Great Psychologist of life. Do you know who He is? Does He know you? Is He helping you make sense out of life? Do not neglect the first and primary relationship in your life!

Another key to happiness in life is the ability to understand pain and suffering, and to finally accept it. Life will deal us pain and suffering. When I ask people about the pain in their life, and why it is there, they typically say, "I don't really know!"

Do you know why Jesus did not go to the Cross kicking and screaming? Because He knew the meaning of the pain and suffering in His life, and He accepted it. So if you asked Jesus, "What is the purpose of your suffering?" He would say, "I have come to serve, to give my life in death so my people can live." We learn from suffering and pain, and we grow. We are purified by the fires of life. We are tempered by the experiences of life. God is molding us, shaping us, bending us for His purpose. Many of us suffer through painful divorces, separation from our children, loss of our mates, and other injustices of life. It is time to stop fighting what life has given you and accept it—and find meaning in what has happened or is happening to you.

Answer this question: "Where would you be without the pain and suffering in your life?"

Some years ago, I became angry at a friend of mine. I had shared with her some of the problems in my life that were causing me pain. After she listened for a while, she replied, "The universe is trying to teach you something, and you haven't learned it yet." I felt insulted. Here I was, a psychologist being analyzed by a non-professional whose advice I didn't ask for. When I recovered from my ego attack, I pondered the question, "What lesson has God been trying to teach me that I have been resisting?" When I was honest with myself, and looked at my unhappiness, I realized I was making some of the same mistakes I had made previously. "How many times would it take for me to learn the lesson, how much pain would I still need to endure before I saw the light?" I reasoned.

By the time I finished my inventory I realized that I wasn't as smart as I thought. Some of my choices were definitely foolish. There were times I misunderstood love and lacked good judgment. It was then I began to change my thinking, which changed my behavior. In the end, I am what I am, I am who I am, not in spite of but because of the painful experiences of life.

If you are still in pain, perhaps you need to ask why!

Remember these few things about happiness:

· Happiness can be yours—you can find it!

· Take up the responsibilities that come to you.

· Align yourself with the will of God as you understand it.

· Never sacrifice personal relationship for "things."

· Make your relationships a priority.

· Seek the most significant relationship of all. He is seeking a relationship with you.

· Give, and serve others!

Questions to Ponder:

1. What makes you happy in your life?
2. What people are you trying to make happy in your life?
3. Are you relationships a priority?

Psychological Insight

Be successful at work, but attend to all of your personal relationships. Seek the primary relationship with Jesus. Understand and seek ways to serve others and understand the meaning of the suffering in your life.

He Taught Us
to Be Thankful

"Lord, please make me humble, and when you do, don't let me know that you did."

In Shakespeare's *King Lear,* the aged king and father is cast out of his kingdom by his daughter. His power stripped away, the king wanders on the gloomy heath, stunned by this act of ingratitude by those he loves. He utters his misfortune to the wind, rain, thunder and lightning and to all who will listen. His words reflect his pain:

> *How sharper than a serpent's tooth it is*
> *To have a thankless child!*
> *Ingratitude, thou marble hearted fiend,*
> *More hideous when thou show'st thee in a child*
> *Than the sea-monster!*[69]

Jesus Ph.D.

In *Gulliver's Travels*, Jonathan Swift tells that in the land of the Lilliputians that ingratitude is reckoned to be a capital crime, and that a man or woman guilty of such a crime is not fit to live. They are considered the enemy of the rest of mankind. The reasoning may sound severe, but perhaps they were right.

Six-year-old Justin was given strict instructions by his mother as he set out for a birthday party of his best friend next door. "Now don't forget to thank Mrs. Henry when you are leaving." Little Justin promised he would. Three hours later when he came home, the first question his mother asked him was, "Did you thank Mrs. Henry?" Mother was dumb-founded that after her lecture the answer was a hesitant, "No." Justin's mother was impatient when she asked "Why not?" Justin said that the party was a lot of fun and he meant to thank her, but as he was leaving the people in front of him, thanked Mrs. Henry, and she replied "Don't mention it." "So I didn't," he replied, very proud of himself.

Jesus had a cure for the ungrateful heart, and it came from His attitude and spirit, which always gave thanks. This is more than a feeling, it is a mind-set, an approach to life. Not only did He teach by His word to give thanks, but one could often find Him giving thanks. In constant contact with His Father, He thanked Him at all times for all things.

One day as Jesus approached a village, ten lepers came out to meet Him. Because they were outcasts, the custom was for them to stay at a distance. Pleading for His mercy, they asked to be healed. Jesus told them to go to the priest and to show themselves, and they would be made whole. On their way to the priest, the lepers were healed. Realizing that he was healed, one delighted leper turned back to thank

Jesus and fall at His feet. Jesus was surprised by two things, first, this man who was thankful was a Samaritan and not a Jew. He was considered a foreigner, or if you please, he was not part of the privileged Jews who believed that they were God's elect. Yet, he was the one who came back with gratitude. The second surprise was that the ten lepers were healed. Jesus asked in amazement, [70]"Were not ten made clean? But the other nine, where are they? Was none found to return and give praise to God except this foreigner?" I believe that Jesus was shocked by this ingratitude and He felt that 10 percent return for the gift He gave to them was not acceptable.

Even Jesus did not like the sting of ingratitude! Jesus must have felt the same when Judas, one of the twelve disciples, betrayed him. Judas lived under the same roof with Jesus, heard the same messages, saw the same miracles, and yet he walked away and sold out the King of Love for thirty pieces of silver. Jesus, no doubt, loved him as much as any disciple, and the same forgiveness was there for him that Simon Peter received. Judas was a "love bandit," just as many in our society are today. He appeared to be loving, but he took and he didn't give back. He gave Jesus the kiss of death. I have always felt a deep sadness over the unfulfilled possibilities of this true story. What was Judas thinking that led him into such darkness?

There was one thank you that Jesus was not pleased about! Jesus tells the parable of a Pharisee who went to the altar of God to pray. He began his prayer by thanking God he was not like other people: thieves, rogues, adulterers, and—seeing the tax collector there—he mentioned the tax collector as well. Jesus said another man went to the same altar and also prayed. He was a tax collector and cried out that he was a sinner. He asked God to bless him in spite of his fallen state. He pictured himself just like other men or worse.

One man was thankful, one man was thankless. One man had a pure heart; one heart was impure, contaminated by his own inflated ego and pride. Jesus obviously wanted to make a point when He told this story!

What is the therapeutic value of saying thank you? First, it keeps us humble. Humility in our present society appears to be a lost virtue. Humility is a state of mind as well as the heart. It deals with our spirit. We let go of our inflated egos and our pride. I use the word "ego" here to mean our selfish pursuits that always start with "I want." Gaining humility is a big dividend for learning how to say thank you. Humility is a rare gift. Many need it, a few have it, almost none seek it.

Also, saying "thank you" leads us to have gratitude, a virtue in itself. Individuals in the presence of a grateful person usually respond in a positive manner. A grateful person is a righteous and wholesome person. Such an individual draws others to themselves. This individual is usually alive to the moment, the precious present. She soaks up the present, and appreciates its preciousness without wanting something else or more. The ungrateful heart always wants something more, something that it doesn't have or that doesn't belong to it. It is always in a state of wanting. This wanting usually creates an unhappiness, a state of restlessness and discontent that leads into dangerous areas.

The third dividend of saying thank you is that it always takes us back to the source of all the gifts in our life. Jesus recognized His Father as the Giver of all good gifts, that is why He constantly said thank you. By going back to the Source, it helps our awareness that we are not the source of the gifts we possess, we are only the recipients. This also keeps us away from false pride.

There is truth in the words, "you are the water but not the river, the oil but not the pipe, the spark but not the energy." This statement has helped me realize that while I am part of the process, I am not the process itself. Within me may be a divine spark, but I am not the divine spark, only the happy receiver.

I am often amused watching others strut around for all the wrong reasons. There are men and women who believe because of their appearance, social status, or material possessions they have something to be boastful about. They flout themselves, believing they are part of a privileged class. In the long run, their attitude usually detracts from any beauty they may possess. Soon, they forget what they have is a gift, a gift which is lent to be used, and which can be taken away at any time.

Consequently, another dividend of staying thankful is the full appreciation of what one has in our life. Such an individual is able to recognize the blessings. We are a spoiled generation, taking things for granted, taking people for granted, and not fully enjoying the assets at our fingertips. It appears to me that our whole society is based on creating want. Television advertising is based on creating a desire for the latest car, the latest best-seller, the most popular cologne, the right toothpaste and the best deodorant. We are saturated not only with these "new" products, but behind them is the message that we cannot be happy or successful without them. It is not that what we already have isn't good, it simply isn't the latest. Creating this "desire" is the basis of our economy, the heart of capitalism.

One of the secrets to happiness in life is not having more but desiring less. Paul, I believe, understood this principle when he declared, "for I have learned to be content with whatever I have. I know what it is to have little, and I know what it is to have plenty." He concluded, "I can do all things through him who strengthens me."[71] Yes, that contentment is within the human heart. Paul possessed this full appreciation of life's blessings.

The Israelites were a people ill-content with what they had. They constantly exhibited an air of ungratefulness. One of their main concerns after coming out of Egypt, was where would they live and how would they eat. [72]God made an arrangement with them: Every day it would rain down bread from heaven, and on the sixth day they would receive a double portion to get them though the Sabbath, which was a day they could not work. So God, faithful to His promise, fed them in the wilderness. Some tried to break the rules, taking more than their share for one day. To their disappointment, it spoiled. Soon there was a faint murmur of discontent. It grew louder every day until it was a shout, and it was directed right at God. The gist of that complaint, "Yes, we have the bread every day, but where's the beef?"

Not even those who came out of Egypt by the mighty hand of God showed much thankfulness at times. Eventually they received a nickname that stuck with them, as being a "stiff-necked people." They came out of Egypt, but it took a long time for the Egypt to come out of them.

A woman I counseled lived in a wealthy suburb of Detroit with her family. She and her husband had lived through the war in Germany and suffered greatly. As Jews, they spent much of the war in hiding, and were always fearful for their lives. There were many times that they did not have proper clothes or food and were often hungry. Finally, they made it to the United States, knowing it was a miracle to be alive. Since that time, life has been good to her and her husband, and they have a successful jewelry business. If I were to characterize her attitude with one word, it would be the word "grateful." Having everything taken away, she appreciates everything she has and takes nothing for granted.

It's her daughter's ungrateful heart that concerns her most. Her daughter has everything she wants and has never suffered difficulties. The monster here is that the more her parents gave her to satisfy her insatiable appetite, the more she wants. The "give me" and "you owe me" attitudes have soured much of their relationship.

Benjamin Franklin once made a list of virtues he would like to attain in his life. He made a separate page listing every virtue, and every day would write down how he did with that particular virtue. One day he showed his list to a friend, who after reading the list informed Franklin that he forgot one important characteristic from his list—humility.

Franklin immediately added it to his important list.

The thankful heart gives and does it willingly; The unthankful heart hoards, afraid it will not receive any more. The humble heart is an open heart, the proud heart is closed. The open and the closed heart is a barometer indicating a person's ability to receive as well as give. The irony here is that whatever you hoard in life, you usually lose or, as with the Israelites, it spoils on you.

Jesus was always thanking His father and began most conversations with His Father that way. But this was more than a greeting, or a nice way to begin His prayers, it was and is the essence of His heart and Spirit. He was thankful for the gifts God had given Him, He was thankful for His disciples, He was thankful for life itself. He was even thankful to serve and give His life for others. Note that He thanked God in the good times as well as the bad. He thanked God when He was on the mountain and especially when He was in the valley. This mind set permeated everything Jesus did during His human walk.

I believe the Great Psychologist knew that the thankful heart was healthy both psychologically and spiritually. Such a heart is open to receive and appreciate all of the wonderful gifts already set aside, just waiting to be poured into our lives. These gifts are imperishable and unlimited by time and space. According to Jesus, the thankful heart is the best way to travel through life. Reach out and take these gifts. They are meant for you!

Questions to Ponder:

1. What are several things in life you are thankful about?

2. What do you still need to work on when it comes to your attitude and spirit?

3. As you reflect on your prayers to God, are they shopping lists of what you want or "thank you" cards ready to send.

Psychological Insight

Jesus declared that the thankful heart is a healthy one. It is most able to give, but also receive the blessing God has intended for him or her. A person with a thankful heart truly sees all of the gifts of life and through humility and thankfulness sustains a wonderful relationship with the Source of all gifts—God.

He Taught Us to Plant

"All work is as seed sown; it grows and spreads
and sows itself anew."
—Thomas Carlyle

Every spring I would seed my garden, and by the end
of the season, I would inevitably end up with a nice crop
of weeds. After repeating this process two years in a row,
someone suggested that I start out with weeds, and see if I
could reverse the process! Fortunately, my green thumb
has improved. Along with watering my seeds, I now talk
to my plants, realizing that they have feelings, love good
music (especially the oldies), and need tender loving care
like the rest of us. Whatever it takes to make them grow!

One of the most significant principles in my
psychology practice is the planting of seeds. It is the
planting of ideas. It is planting new patterns of behavior.

Why don't all the seeds grow? Sometimes, the seeds
are planted before we are ready or mature enough to let
them grow. Other times, we take the positive, good, seed
we receive and put it back into environments where the

new isn't welcomed or supported by those around us. We often underestimate the dysfunctional and the negative in our surroundings, negative that will quench the good, not by accident but on purpose.

A woman I once counseled, came from a background of deep-seated co-dependency and low self-esteem. She decided she was no longer going to be a door mat for her friends and family, nor was she going to be quiet, afraid of hurting someone's feelings while her own feelings were being violated. The meek little mouse was about to roar.

Her mate was threatened by her new changes, and tried to sabotage her efforts by discouraging her from going to therapy anymore. "I like the old you," he declared. Certainly he did! He could still control his spouse, stay in his comfort zone, and not be accountable for his actions. She continued to nurture her "seed," however. The marriage survived, but not without a great deal of growing pains.

It may take years for the seed to grow, and the one who plants may not be the one who nurtures the growth. The one who nurtures the growth may not be the one who harvests the crop. Together, many people may take part in the entire process of planting and reaping.

At other times, the seeds may not germinate because of our laziness. It takes effort to stick to good ideas and new patterns, or a challenging plan for our lives. Effort is equal to work, and in this case, hard work. It is interesting that M. Scott Peck in his book, *The Road Less Traveled*, defines the original sin that occurred in the Garden of Eden as laziness. Adam and Eve took time to listen to the derogatory information offered by the fallen angel concerning God, but never once made a single effort to go and check it out with God or even talk to Him about it.

Instead, they both were too lazy to do what could have changed the impending tragedy. Their laziness cost them the seed of life and the gift of eternal life that God had planted within them.

Jesus knew the importance of planting, and mentioned it several times in His stories. One parable He told was about a sower who went out to plant seed. The seed fell on four different areas: the path, the rocks, the thorns, and finally, good soil. None of the seed survived except what fell on good soil. The seed that fell on the path was trampled, and the birds came and ate it. The seed that fell on the rocks died because of the lack of moisture. The seed on the thorns was literally choked out by the thorns. The seed that found good soil not only grew, but astonishingly grew with great abundance—a hundredfold.

What did this story of planting and the seed have to do with real life? Jesus did not leave this interpretation to the disciples. He wanted to make sure we got it right.

Wherever Jesus went, He planted seeds, which are ideas about His kingdom and His work.

· He planted a seed with Nicodemus

· He planted a seed with the woman at the well.

· He planted a seed with Zaccheus

· He planted a seed with Mary and Martha about eternal life.

The Great Psychologist sows the seed, and the negativism of our world sows confusion and chaos. This book does not discuss whether or not you believe Satan to be a real person. I am convinced that anyone, anywhere, at any time, who underestimates the negative and the evil in our world is a blind fool. Jesus apparently believed that evil was personified by one person, a fallen angel who comes to take the seed away. He boldly stated that he is "the father of lies." Whether you accept this or not, the truth is the seed still is eaten up by the negativism that attacks our lives.

Negativism is often dangerously lurking in those who are close to us, whispering adverse messages in our ears. Those not well-grounded in truth and morality have their roots just inches below the surface. These are shallow people who may mean well, but when the storms of life come, and persist, they cannot survive because their roots don't grow deep. The seed among the thorns cannot survive because it is choked out. In real life, the seed is choked by wrong priorities and wrong focus, according to Jesus . The cares, the pleasures, and the riches so preoccupy those receiving the seed that it is choked for lack of time and energy. Look around—the Great Psychologist knows our present society quite well!

Whatever doesn't allow the seed to grow kills the seed and the dream within us that seeks the light of the Son, to grow a hundredfold. The seed not only grew in the good soil, but those who heard, and represented the good soil, nurtured the seed and gave it what it needed to grow. Jesus said they have a good and honest heart. In the time of Jesus, the biggest deterrent for the seed to flourish among the religious leaders was their pride and their belief that they already had all of the answers of life. Consequently, they crossed their arms and closed their minds and hearts. Jesus warned His disciples, [73]"beware of the leaven of the Pharisees, which is hypocrisy." By this he was speaking of their toxic teachings and their narrow thinking.

How can we interpret what the Great Psychologist may be saying to us about the seeds of life planted in our life? Human nature has not changed that much, we are still hindering the seed from growing today. We are still allowing negativism in our lives to steal the eternal seeds. Our instant society of quick fixes and impatience is still not giving the seeds in our life time to take root. Our focus on the busy, temporary, world of perishable things, such as riches, everyday concerns, as well as pleasure, still monopolize us and choke out the lasting imperishable seed.

Then, we wonder, why are we psychologically sick? We question why we are faced with a generation of addiction. We wonder what has robbed us of our freedom. We don't have to go far to find the answers!

Human nature has not changed. It's only old problems in new clothes. We are still lazy, we are still busy with the wrong things. We are still caught up in our pride and false egos, and we still believe that we already possess the truth, thus holding back the insights that knock upon the doors of our hearts.

As a young boy in the 14th Century, Marco Polo would sit at the feet of his father, enchanted by stories of strange people, exotic lands, and unusual customs. His father, a successful Venetian merchant, told him stories of people with yellow skin and a certain slant to their eyes. Marco Polo's father was an adventurous man who had traveled as far as Peking in search of merchandise to sell, and reportedly he even traded with those in China. At that time in Europe, the Europeans were fascinated by new discoveries from the East, especially when traders brought back fine silks.

The seed was planted in his mind—and the seed grew. When his father began talking about going back to the land of Confucious, young Marco Polo begged his father to take him along.

So, he went on the journey of his life. He was excited by everything—the burning oil (petroleum), the peaks of the Himalayas, and the great cities of China. What he saw was more fascinating than his father had led him to believe.

Young Marco Polo served in the court of Kublai Khan for many years, and did not return home until the age of forty-one. As a result of his extensive journey, he wrote, *The Book of Marco Polo,* a fabulous description of his varied adventures. It is still the classic tour book of all time.

Planting seeds is important work. For example, as long as I can remember, I have been fascinated by cars. In the early 1970s, I was just learning about them. One day I ventured into a dealership that specialized in British automobiles. In the showroom was a sporty MG convertible, as well as a Triumph. In the middle of the showroom was a beautifully-displayed Silver Shadow Rolls Royce.

I asked one of the salespeople if I could sit in the vehicle, and he hesitated before saying if I didn't have anything sharp in my pocket that would tear the leather it would be okay. The smell of the leather and the look of the burled walnut was magnificent. Still curious, I asked to see the engine compartment. Suddenly, a disdainful grin came over his face, and then he politely said in his British accent, "No, I couldn't possibly do that!" When I asked him why not, he repeated his response and walked away.

Not easily discouraged, I soon found the manager whose name was Robert, and I asked him why I couldn't see the engine compartment. He simply smiled at me with a sheepish grin, and said that his salesman didn't believe I had enough money to buy the car, and so didn't want to show it to me. The salesman thought it was a waste of time. Robert, however, was eager to please, and he immediately took me to the front of the Rolls Royce and opened the hood, exposing a beautiful shiny display of magnificent engineering.

"So, why are you showing me the engine compartment?" I gratefully asked.

"Because I am planting seeds," he replied with a slight smile on his face. He continued, "I would open this hood for a boy who is twelve! Because, someday, he will be back."

In the years since that experience, I have come to realize that Robert understood a lot about planting, and much more about the psychology of men and their toys.

The Great Psychologist has already planted seeds in your life. He is still planting and will plant until the day you stand before Him. He loves planting seeds. What kind of soil are you providing for them?

Questions to Ponder:

1. What seeds are being planted in your life by others?
2. What seeds are you planting in your life?
3. What are you doing about the weeds in your life?

Psychological Insight

The planting of seeds is important to the process of life. Be aware of what will attempt to steal and destroy the divine seed. It is rewarding to watch our seeds grow, not only in our lives, but in the lives of our loved ones and those around us. It is our responsibility to provide good soil for the good things in our life to grow and to stay focused on them. Be attentive to your garden of life!

THE POWER OF RELATIONSHIPS

He Taught That Love May Be Difficult

In Him, the greatest gift of all was given— unconditional love

I met Dr. Margaret during the summer when I was a student minister in Chicago, although her reputation preceded our acquaintance. One hot July day, she invited my family to her home outside of Chicago. Dr. Margaret looked like the stereotypical retired school teacher. Behind her horn rimmed glasses, her warm eyes were intense. Her soft gray hair caught the rays of the summer sun. Her face was wrinkled with character and wisdom, while her aged eyes that drew me to her looked as if they held a thousand intriguing stories. We sat across from each other in her backyard, each with a glass of lemonade in hand, and what unfolded was a remarkable story of love.

She began by telling me that she had ventured to India as a medical missionary in the early 1920's, with a Bible in one hand and her black medical bag in the other. In her

Jesus Ph.D.

heart was a deep faith in God and her mission. She pitched her tent at the edge of the desert, ready to go to work, but to her disappointment many who needed her medical assistance were suspicious of this newcomer from the West.

Of all the groups she encountered, she said the lepers were the most fascinating. Everyday they would come and stand a safe distance from her tent. They looked lonely and helpless and were outcasts from their society. Everyday she put out bread for them. Everyday they refused—even in their tremendous hunger—to come and take it. Yet, each day their hunger brought them closer to her tent. The lepers and Dr. Margaret carefully watched each other, studying each other's habits and actions, yet keeping that safe distance.

Then one day there was a breakthrough. Their hunger finally drove them to the very door of her tent, and they timidly picked up the bread and stuffed it into their mouths. But it was the encounter between them that was amazing. For some unknown, unpremeditated, reason, Dr. Margaret reached out and took the hand of one of the lepers and examined her diseased hand. No words were exchanged between them, but a tear streamed down the face of the young missionary and fell onto the dirt of the hot desert. She was surprised to look up and discover a tear also running from the eye of this young rejected leper. The next day a similar experience occurred.

From that time on Dr. Margaret's reputation spread. She had dared to touch a leper and thus endangered her own life. Remember there was no cure for leprosy at that time. After that incident Dr. Margaret was known as "The Leper Lady," a name that stuck with her all during her missionary days. The barriers between the lepers and Dr.

196

Margaret were broken, and she spent many years in India successfully spreading her love and the love of God.

The spell of Dr. Margaret's storytelling was broken when my wife came to tell me our children were tired and we needed to take them home. The images of India quickly vanished, and I was brought back to the reality of Dr. Margaret's backyard near Chicago. As I looked at my watch, I was surprised to discover that three hours had passed in what seemed to be a brief moment. A sense of awe came over me, and I was aware I had been in the presence of a pure soul.

As I drove home that evening, I was pensive. I thought about how universal the language of love is. Dr. Margaret did not understand the language of the lepers; they did not understand her spoken words. Yet on that hot summer day in India, the lepers and Dr. Margaret touched each other. It was the beginning of the most fascinating pilgrimages of her life. Her story affirms that love doesn't always need words; deeds stand above any human utterance.

She had given them a great gift! She had given herself. They gave her as great a gift in return.

Jesus challenges everyone to expand their love, to enlarge the circle of love, to include not exclude. Including others who we don't know well, or don't like isn't easy! A client of mine showed up at a singles' group at which I spoke. Before I began my talk, I introduced her as a friend of mine and asked the group to give her a warm welcome. They all said in unison, "Welcome Stacey!" as was their custom. As I was leaving the meeting, I noticed that most people were talking and socializing, but no one was talking to Stacey. I felt a pain rip through me as I identified with what she might be feeling. They were friendly, but among themselves. Rejection is such a difficult experience to live through. I thought to myself, "If only they would make a bigger circle to include Stacey."

The life Stacey has lead so far has been difficult. When she first came for therapy, she was deeply depressed. Her life seemed to be going in circles and nothing she did seemed to be working. She felt lonely and isolated. Two years before she came to therapy, her husband left her for another coworker. Shortly after that her mother, her only real confidante, died. In 1989, her sixteen-year-old son Jerry died from muscular dystrophy. Two years later, her son Billy died from the same illness.

Stacey was despondent. She felt lost. If I said that she felt abandoned, it would be a gross understatement. Words were not strong enough to describe her pain. She felt all the people she loved had left her. These experiences in life would be difficult enough for anyone to bear, but for Stacey there was much more.

Stacey was the youngest in her family, and the rest of her siblings were grown up and out of the house during most of her childhood. Her father, an ardent workaholic, was not emotionally available for her. Her older brothers and sister were critical of her and everything she tried to do, and soon Stacey became the black sheep of the family. By the time she was an adult, her self-esteem was at zero. She became codependent in order to get the love she needed for her life. She also became a doormat for everyone, especially her ex-husband who also tried to control her life.

She would often drive to my office in a car that I was convinced was held together by wires and bandages, but every Tuesday she would faithfully show up for her appointment at 11 AM. Stacey's persistent faith in God wouldn't let her give up, and God did not give up on Susan.

The road to well-being has been a slow, difficult journey for Stacey. However, perhaps this is the best kind of lasting growth. Today, Stacey, age 41, is losing weight, has her own apartment, drives a late model car, and goes country-line dancing twice a week. She is a very lovable person, and to see her progress reminds me of the mission in my work as a psychologist. Her happiness has no price tag. She is getting married within the year

Perhaps the greatest challenge Jesus gives us is in the area of love. He urges us to not only love, but to love the unlovable. To put it in different words, expand your capacity to love. Love what is difficult to love, love what may not be beautiful, love the unlovable. Jesus declared, "If you love those who love you what credit is that to you? For even sinners love those who love them." Then He gives us the supreme test, [74]"Love your enemies, do good to those who hate you."

Jesus was often criticized for loving the unlovable. He was frequently found on the wrong side of town, talking and eating with prostitutes, the poor, tax collectors, Gentiles, and those who were considered inappropriate. He visited and talked to the politically incorrect. These efforts of Jesus were not random, they were purposely planned. On one occasion, the Pharisees and Scribes came complaining to His disciples, and asked this question, "Why do you eat and drink with tax collectors and sinners?" Here is Jesus' answer, [75]"Those who are well have no need of a physician, but those who are sick; I have come to call not the righteous but sinners to repentance." Jesus continued throughout His earthly life to associate with, accept, and love those considered by others the outcast and the unlovely of society.

If He physically walked among us today, the Great Psychologist would be assaulted for this same principle of love. If love is easy, perhaps it isn't love. The words and life of Jesus were put to love's greatest test. He proved worthy of being our model.

As I write this book, a great deal of attention is being given to the school massacre in Littleton, Colorado. What a horrendous tragedy! It has raised some haunting questions. In the days ahead, I believe that it will be revealed that dozens of people ignored countless signals sent out by these two young boys who did the killing. I believe that we will discover that they felt rejected and unloved by many of their classmates. One cannot help but have compassion for those who lost loved ones and students and parents who lived through the pain and trauma of that ordeal. However, can we feel compassion and love for these young men who, while they are totally responsible for their actions, must have been driven by such dark deep emotions to do that which is so "inhuman?" What elicited such hatred for their classmates and such self-hatred? How big is our circle of love? Can we love these two young men? Are we wise enough to avoid the future Littletons?

I prefer to like the clients who come to me. It makes the sessions go easier and more quickly, rather than being tedious and drawn-out. It is one thing for the client to look at his watch, but when I am constantly looking at the clock—I know I am in trouble!

Joshua, a man in his middle-thirties, was a client I had difficulty liking. He did everything he could to make our sessions difficult right from the beginning. After our first stormy session, I informed him that I could not accept him as a client, I wasn't sure our time together could be productive. His language was abusive and he was very cocky. He began his session by informing me even though he was here because he was in trouble with the law he didn't do anything wrong. From there he attempted to berate the court and the judge, who in Joshua's opinion, was a jerk. He also made it clear that any abuse he had given his wife was her own fault, because of her bad attitude.

When I told him at the end of the first session that I was not going to make another appointment for him, he surprised me. All of his defenses came down and he pleaded with me to continue with him. He was so adamant that I told him I would think about it.

I had the weekend to think about the case and I decided again not to take the case. However, every time I came to that conclusion there was a nagging feeling that came over me, plus a little whisper that accompanied the feeling, saying "Take this case!" I reasoned that there were other individuals out there who could help, and yet there was this persistent conflict. My head said "No" and my heart said, "Yes." I put it out of my mind and thought the whole incident was forgotten. However, Thursday Joshua called and left a message on my answering machine, "Can I make an appointment with you to come in Monday of next week?"

I called him back to definitely tell him of my decision. By the time I got off the phone, we had agreed for him to come in the next Monday to begin his treatment. Something, or Someone, I realized stopped me from turning him away. I reasoned, "If the Great Psychologist wants me to see him, I know He has a plan." But, "Oh my, what a pain this was going to be," I thought to myself. I was not disappointed. Joshua continued to challenge me and my authority in almost every session.

One day when my secretary had gone early and he was sitting in the waiting room, I discovered that he had purposely listened to part of someone's session. When I asked him why, he told me he wanted to see how I interacted with another client. I won't share with you my response to him but it was very stern. On another occasion, when I had to leave the room momentarily he let me know that he was eager to get his fingers on his file. Fortunately, I had already learned to always to take my file with me! On such occasions with him, I always asked him to leave the office as well.

One day our sessions came to a head. He shared with me that it would be easy for him to find out where I lived and my home telephone number and if he wanted to, he could stalk me. Then he told me that he often thought of ways to manipulate me during our sessions together. He complained about the money I charged for his sessions, even though he paid a modest fee. He resisted telling me about his past, and tried to block me from probing into it by saying it wasn't important anymore. His language continued to be abusive at times, and he still attempted to cross boundaries.

I went back and prayed about Joshua, asking the Great Psychologist why he had come to me, and what possible good I could do for him. I could not see how I could help someone who didn't want to change. Always I received the same answer, "Don't give up on Joshua." I discovered I was dreading our sessions together, and relieved when they were over.

Then, for ten days, I didn't hear from or see Joshua. He had violated his probation and was in jail for threatening his estranged wife. My report to the probation department was candid, and probably contributed to his sentence!

The conditions in the jail for Joshua were unpleasant. He didn't have a place to sleep and several inmates harassed him, both sexually and physically. He only took four showers while he was there.

He called me as soon as he was out, and asked if he could see me as soon as possible. I was surprised when he came in with a smile on his face. He claimed he was glad to see me. I surprised myself, I told him I was happy to see him, and after I said it, I realized that I meant it. He shared with me that he had a spiritual experience while in jail. God had come to him in a powerful way and told him the people around him were trying to help him, he needed to let them. He realized that he was not getting out of life what he wanted because he was going at it in the wrong way. He also felt remorse for many of the things he had done that had caused people pain, and he stated that in some way God made him feel that pain while he was in jail. He shared that he had come to believe that many of the things that I was counseling him about were true, but that he had been fighting me, because trusting anyone was a problem with him.

He told me he was ready to listen.

To tell you I almost fell off my chair, would be a gross understatement. I was doubtful, amazed, dumbfounded, and delighted all at the same time. After that session, he asked if he could hug me. I immediately blurted out, "No!" I was not ready for that quick a transformation.

Do you think Joshua was genuine? Do you think he stayed on his new course?

In the sessions that followed I discovered why power and control were so important to him. During most of his life he felt powerless. Joshua's father was extremely abusive and would beat him for no apparent reason. When he came home intoxicated, he was a mean drunk and he would take it out on Sarah, his faithful wife. When young

Joshua would stand between them in order to protect his mother, and was beaten as well. This abusive experience started when Joshua was four years old and ended when he was sixteen. At that age, his father left, abandoning the family physically and financially. Joshua tried to support the family the best he could, but earned little money most of his teenage and early adult years. During his sessions when he spoke of his father, he would often become extremely angry, and the years of pent-up poison would come spewing out. Often he would ask, "Why was he so mean to me? Why did he beat me for no reason?" While at these times, he would become tearful, I knew that he would not cry in my presence. It would be a sign of weakness.

For most of Joshua's life, he felt he was powerless over the negative experiences that he had lived through. Depression and the feeling of being a victim were his constant companions, which he camouflaged well. However, on the inside he was often fearful and crying.

Joshua did stay on course!

One year ago from this writing, he finished his program with me. He totally reconciled with his wife and his eight-year-old son. He has learned to be a good father, something he did not have modeled for himself. He finally got out of the cycle of legal problems, and has the psychological tools to stay out. He comes in occasionally to maintain his new course. He is doing well, he claims he is happy and he looks happy. I am delighted to tell you that so persistent was Joshua about change that this story has a happy ending.

I wish I could tell you that Joshua is an isolated case, rare rather than common, but I would not be telling you the truth. We are surrounded by so many Joshuas!

As I write these words, I am smiling. How easy it would have been to have taken the well-worn path and to have walked away from Joshua. How easy it was not to love him, but then I would have been just like the rest of those who cluttered his life. Not loving and accepting Joshua is what he expected! Loving Joshua pushed me out of my comfort zone more than once, but I learned something about myself, and something about what the difficult side of love is all about.

In the end, I realized more than ever that love is the transforming power of life. Without it our lives are nothing. Love is the catalyst for rebirth and renewal, and its touch is what can heal our ugliness.

I tell this story as a challenge for each of us to expand our concept of love: to love the poor of heart, the weak, the unlovable, and those who are broken by life.

Today, we often ask, "What would Jesus do?"

My answer is, "He would have us love those who are hard to love!"

Questions To Ponder:

1. Who in your life is most difficult to love?
2. How have you responded to this person?
3. Name some concrete things you will do to show your love to someone who is unlovable today.

Psychological Insight

Broaden your concept of love and stop doing what is easy. Stretch your circle to include the unlovable—looking beyond the externals and seeing each individual as a child of God. Within each one there is something beautiful to love.

He Empowered People, Especially Women

"To take the significant women out of your life, is to have a life void of beauty and love."

As you read the pages of the New Testament, it appears that something new and different is happening in the way women are treated. It's much different than in the first pages of the book of Genesis, where we find Adam blaming Eve for the trouble in the Garden of Eden. Adam was definitely not going to take responsibility for eating the fruit of the forbidden tree—he said it was Eve's fault. Because of the Eve's transgression, God declares, [62]"I will greatly increase your pangs in childbearing."

This blaming others instead of taking responsibility was only a prelude of what is still going on in our society today. How different we are from President Harry Truman who had a sign on his desk which read, "The buck stops here." These words are seldom heard in our contemporary society.

Jesus, Ph.D., empowered women. Empowerment is one of the dynamic gifts of therapy which gives others the power they need to live life. Jesus had numerous encounters with women during his earthly existence, rich and poor women alike were part of His inner circle and faithful supporters of His work and mission.

The New Testament begins with women taking center stage as the magnificent news of the birth of a God's Son is given to a young virgin. The angel Gabriel is assigned this task, and announces, [77]"And now, you will conceive in your womb and bear a son, and you will name him Jesus." The angel makes it perfectly clear this is the most significant person in history. In response, Mary declares, [78]"Here am I, the servant of the Lord; let it be with me according to your word." A special, yet ordinary woman is singled out for a significant role in history.

Gabriel then appears to another woman, [79]Elizabeth who is advanced in age. He announces that she will give birth "And you, child, will be called the prophet of the Most High; . . ." Her son, John the Baptist, would be the forerunner of Jesus. The New Testament opens its pages with two faithful women who will give birth to the most significant men in all history. Did they feel empowered? Absolutely, and they used their power wisely and blessed God for it.

During His life, Jesus enjoyed the company of women. One illustration of this is that Jesus constantly retreats to the home of Mary and Martha, where He enjoys their support and friendship. This seems to be His favorite place to relax from the intensity of His mission.

Another time, Jesus' mother, who believes in Him and knows His true identity, says to Him at the marriage of Cana,[80] "They have no wine." Thus He performs His first miracle encouraged by His mother. Mary realizes that He has the power of God within Him.

Yet again, Jesus encounters the woman at the well and asks her for water. Then He invites her to drink of eternal water so that she will never thirst again. His disciples are frustrated that He has ignored local customs to talk to her. Later, He is moved by the woman who anoints Him with costly oils and declares that she has done a beautiful thing for Him. He heals the woman who has hemorrhaged for twelve years and informs her that her faith has healed her.

Jesus forgives the woman taken in adultery and challenges her to go and sin no more. He cries at the tomb of Lazarus, the brother of Mary and Martha, and tells the two women their brother will live again. Then Pontius Pilate's wife tells him, [81]"Have nothing to do with that innocent man for today I have suffered a great deal because of a dream about Him." Pilate plows ahead anyway, knowing Jesus is innocent, yet giving the order to crucify Him despite his wife's warning.

It is a woman at the tomb who first recognizes Him after his resurrection, in contrast to a doubting man who needs to put his finger into Jesus' wounds before he believes. Yes, women played an integral part of His life and His work, and continue to do so. He knew who they were and loved them. He knows and He loves women today.

Jesus has written a new page in history for women and He has liberated them, especially from cultural bondage. There is no male chauvinism that is ever evident by His words or actions. He treats women with love and respect and not as second-class citizens. He sees them as equal partners in His work and kingdom. At this point

Jesus is definitely breaking ranks with the contemporary Jewish society in which He lived and moving in a new, exciting, direction for women.

It is always exciting when I see others empowered. Elizabeth Barrett Browning of England was such a woman. Her father forbade any of his twelve children to marry. In 1838 she was seriously ill as the result of a broken blood vessel. Two years later her oldest brother drowned, leaving her with a grief that lasted all of her life. She seemed to be destined to the life of an invalid. Then, she met Robert Browning who, after reading and admiring her publication of 1844 *Poems,* began corresponding with her. He was a persistent suitor. In 1846, they were secretly married and she was whisked away by her husband. They traveled throughout Europe and she made a miraculous recovery in spite of her frailty. At the age of forty-three she was robust enough to give birth to a son. She lived until 1861, empowered by a husband who believed in her and by this new ingredient in her life—love.

One of my clients, Laura, was married to John for ten years, in which he convinced her that she had a serious psychological problem, not him. This is a typical tactic used by controlling, abusive men. He was flirtatious with other women who called the house and talked to him for hours while she was ignored. He gave them expensive gifts and accepted gifts from them. When she explained to him that she was jealous by this female attention, he criticized her for being overly-sensitive. When he humiliated her in front of his family during family get-togethers, he minimized it, saying he didn't mean anything by it. She had a lot of support from family and friends, who were constantly bewildered that she accepted such abuse.

Finally, one day she got angry! First, she got angry with her husband and came to the conclusion that the emotional abuse was longer lasting than any physical abuse, because it bruised her heart. Then she got mad at herself saying, "How could I have put up with this garbage all these years?" Then she announced to her husband that slavery was over and she could no longer live with the same rules. She went for help to break her own negative patterns of behavior.

John never responded to her in a positive way. He refused to change. He is still abusive, but now he is the only one who has to live with it. One of his last messages to Laura was that she could not make it without a man. This time she didn't buy his program.

Laura has come to enjoy what the Great Psychologist wanted for her all along, to fully live as a human being, knowing her numerous possibilities and living out her dreams. She feels empowered by the new information and insights she has learned. She is not about to give them up for anyone. She now wonders why she stayed so long.

To empower, doesn't mean to use the power for someone else but to give them the power to use for themselves. Once they use the tools that work, the feeling of empowerment grows. These tools may be translated into a new idea, a new insight, or a different way of doing the usual. It may be a different understanding of a problem you are facing. When these tools are used a wonderful marvelous thing occur—the person using the tools feels a burst of energy. A new pattern is formed, one that works. Soon the person begins to reason, "Gee, if that worked in that area, maybe it can work over here." A person feeling empowered is more apt to be able to move away from depression and feeling like a victim to new freedom. Their self-esteem usually increases. As one can see, empowering others has several nice dividends. It is always rewarding to see others take control of their life again.

I remember Jane asking me for suggestions on how to discipline her ten-year-son, or better yet, ideas to get him to cooperate with her. I gave her several tips which she went home and tried over the weekend. When she came back, she was smiling. More than one of my suggestions that she tried had worked. She seemed surprised, saying, "Why didn't I try those sooner?" Jane not only felt empowered, but she was ready to move with her empowerment into new areas.

Jesus as a man, interestingly enough, possessed what we traditionally have termed to be female characteristics. Jesus showed a sensitivity to the needs of others, he was a great listener, and He was in touch with his feelings and showed his emotion. He did this unashamedly during his earthly life and without apology. Male or female, these are great characteristics for anyone to possess. Jesus was ahead of His time in defining the "new" man, in fact, we are just now catching up with Him.

The best part of this truth is that the living Jesus still exhibits these nurturing characteristics today toward every individual who calls upon His name.

Jesus loves women. He believes in them, and they played an important part in His life on earth. Jesus set women free from the prejudice and misconceptions which held them captive, and by doing so He empowered them. When it came to women, Jesus broke ranks, and made it clear they are a significant part of His kingdom.

Jesus empowered women in His time. Jesus empowers women today!

Questions to Ponder

1. What women have been significant in your life?
2. If you are a woman, what individuals in your life have understood you and empowered you?
3. If you are a woman, who have you empowered?

Psychological Insight

From the beginning of his earthly work, women have always been a significant part of Jesus' world. He has always sought to understand them, to give them the tools they need to live life, and to honor their special place in His kingdom. Jesus loves and empowers women today! He delights in empowering you!

> *Jesus never said,*
> *You shall not be tempted,*
> *You shall not be depressed,*
> *You shall not be troubled,*
> *He did say,*
> *You shall not be overcome!*

He Taught That Love
Is the Priority

"I don't care what good you do in life, others
many see it as a great thing; if it is not
motivated by love, it is worthless"
—The apostle Paul, (a paraphrase of
I Corinthians 13)

On April 20, 1999, two teenage gunmen stormed
Columbine High School with assault weapons and bombs.
As they swept through the school, they killed twelve
students, injured dozens more and then killed themselves. One
sophomore, Patrick Simington, recalls the phrase on the
classroom video screen after the morning announcements that
read, "I bet you wish you weren't here today!" Who wouldn't
agree, especially with what was about to unfold in the next few
hours.

When the gunfire began, William "Dave" Sanders, a
computer and business teacher, led a dozen students to
safety. As he came down the hallway, he was shot twice in

the chest. He stumbled into a second floor science room with his students still following him. Blood was streaming from his wounds, and his faithful students tried feverishly to stop the bleeding by ripping their clothing into bandages. Sanders kept trying to get up, trying to lead the students out of the building, but he was too weak, too fatally wounded.

Help did not come until four hours later. Sanders was conscious, and knew he wouldn't make it. He asked a student to take his pictures of his children out of his wallet and show them to him. The last words on his lips were, "Tell them I love them." He died a few short breaths later.

His students will remember the love of Dave Sanders. He will live in their memories forever. He gave them the most valuable gift he possessed: his life.

Jesus said [81]"No greater love has any man than this, that a man lay down his life for his friends." Soon, Jesus would prove by His own sacrificial love that He possessed this "greater love." He set the standard for love, and then He fulfilled it.

Jesus, the Great Psychologist, was never given the title, The King of Love," but the title fits Him well. Not only is He the supreme example of love, but He encourages us to love each other. To love is more than a suggestion; it is His commandment and the psychological key to happiness. There is no happiness without love. Love is the core of our well-being. Love is what we are, and what we are meant to do in our lives. God is love, and we are created in His image. Consequently, it is accurate to say that love is our essence. If we do not love, we deny our destiny and our own purpose. Then love will always elude us.

In my course of studies at Hope College, Western Seminary and then the Center for Humanistic Studies, I have been disappointed and at the same time surprised that so little was said about love. Never in nine years of higher education did I ever take a course about "love." There were none offered! Perhaps, it is assumed that in our present society, we know about love, when in fact, we are naïve and ignorant about the greatest force in life. If we knew so much about love, we wouldn't be leaving behind a junkyard of broken relationships and shattered dreams. The truth is, no one has ever been happy who was not loved, and no one has ever been happy who did not love. How important is love to your psychological health? It is everything! It is my firm belief we can never know enough about love.

It is obvious that Jesus loved during His earthly life. He loved His human parents, Mary and Joseph. He loved His disciples and especially the disciple, John. He loved the impulsive Peter. He loved Lazarus and wept at his grave. When He stood outside Jerusalem, and looked down on the city, He wept for those within. The compassion He felt for the crowd that came to hear Him teach, and was hungry, was a demonstration of the practical side of His love. His forgiveness of those who crucified Him was also a powerful sign of His love.

Someone has stated "If Love is not unconditional, it ends up to be manipulation." The problem in our society is that we have an abundance of such conditional love; love with requirements and agendas. Love in our world should be labeled, "Fragile, handle with care." Traditionally, mothers give to their children unconditional love. Fathers have traditionally given to their children conditional love—withholding it until their son or daughter proves themselves to be worthy. I am always amused at mothers who rave about their newborn baby who can only poop at one end and burp at the other! Yet to them, that baby is the most precious gift in the world. Fortunately, men and women today are breaking out of these traditional, stereotypical categories.

The love which Jesus has for us is not conditional in any way. It is of a higher order. He is the Alpha and Omega of love—the beginning and the end.

Efforts to define love have all come up short. Shakespeare once said that love is not time's fool. It does not diminish with the passage of time. Carl Rogers defines love in a therapeutic setting as "unconditional high regard." I believe that love for another person is an extension of ourselves, to desire the highest good for the one we love. This is selfless love, rather than selfish love. Although we cannot see love because it is an invisible dynamic force as mysterious as the Spirit which Jesus talked about with Nicodemus, we do see what love does, and the rewards of love. So this invisible, intangible, powerful force is at work among us.

The Great Psychologist has much to say about love. The first, as I shared earlier, is sacrificial love, such as the Columbine teacher showed for his students, and Jesus gave to the world. The second is our love for God. In response to a lawyer who asked, [82]"Teacher, which commandment in the Law is the greatest?," Jesus said, "You shall love the Lord your God with all your heart, and with all your soul, and with all your mind." This is the greatest commandment. And the second is similar: "You shall love your neighbor as yourself. On these two commandments hang all the Law and the prophets."

We have become so accustomed to this significant summary of love that we may not realize that the Pharisees and Scribes spent endless effort and time over a period of several hundred years interpreting the meaning of the Ten Commandments. They accumulated more than 600 interpretations on what the Law meant as it was translated into the everyday life of the common Jew. Each interpretation was specific interpretation of one of the Ten Commandments. This body of work became known as the Talmud.

An example of one interpretation was the commandment of keeping the Sabbath holy. It was interpreted to mean that one could not venture more than a mile from home on the Sabbath. Jews could get around the requirement by carrying a loaf of bread, and putting a piece of bread down every mile they walked. After all, bread was where your home was! These rules were laid down by the same authorities who constantly criticized Jesus for healing on the Sabbath, because healing was considered work. Jesus, undoubtedly, believed that the results of their efforts were cumbersome and restricting. Their results were legalistic and lost the spirit of the Law. Their new rules and principles had become a burdensome religion unto itself.

Jesus took all of their rules, regulations, and interpretations and boiled them down to one single word, "love." Love is the common denominator. Imagine that! Six hundred interpretations reduced down to one word— "love." The Scribes and Pharisees who heard Him utter this simplified version were not happy campers about what he was doing with their sacred efforts.

Jesus said love needs to flow in two directions. First, love must flow vertically toward the Highest Power of the Universe. Then, love must flow in a horizontal direction, toward those around us. Love forms the spirit of the Law and motivates its observance. Notice how we are to love, in total, with all our heart, with all our mind, and with all our soul. Jesus is asking for an all-out effort; an effort which will encompass all of our focus, and all of our energy.

This is to be a love which springs forth from our emotions, a love which directs our thoughts, a love which possesses our actions. When we love horizontally, we love ourselves and our neighbor. Jesus assumed that we would love ourselves. Too many have confused self-love as selfishness, rather than realizing that the Great Psychologist knew this was the key to psychological health. The word "all" in Jesus' words is a big key here. When we love with all we have, we could say that we hold nothing back. It also means that we love with intensity, focus and total commitment. It doesn't take a rocket scientist or even a psychologist to realize that when you love in this particular way, whether it is love of God, mother, father, sister, brother, your children, or your mate, you will get great results.

The truth is, we often stumble into life in a half-hearted way, and we love the same way. Often we walk around wondering why things aren't going the way we planned for our relationships and our life. On a regular basis, I bring this lack of totality in our efforts to love to the attention of those who seek insights on why their life isn't going well. Everyone needs this kind of reminder.

Jesus also declared, [83]"Love one another as I have loved you." This is a significant bond between those who give an unselfish love for each other in a selfish and self-serving world. The powerful testimony of the early Christians to an unbelieving world was "see how they love one another."

I often wonder how well we are doing today, this very moment, with this principle of love!

It has been said that Gandhi attended a Christian Church for several Sundays while he was in South Africa. However, he came to the conclusion that the congregation was not particularly religous. They did not serem to him to be very devout, but were going to church for the recreation and conformity of what was expected of them. Consequently, he never went back, nor did he pursue the Christian faith. Unfortunately, in that little gathering of Christians, he did not see the powerful, dynamic bond of love which Jesus said what set them apart from the world.

The apostle Paul defines the principles of love in 1 Corinthians 13, when he says that all deeds are meaningless unless they are motivated by love. The gifts we give either to God or those around us need to come from a heart of love. Otherwise, they are empty. Then Paul defines the behavior of love. While he was not trying to give us an exhaustive description, he does give us a benchmark to measure all love. Here are a few of the characteristics of love:

· Love is very patient

· Love is kind

· Love is not jealous

· Love is not boastful

· Love is not conceited

· Love is not rude

· Love is not selfish

· Love does not have a temper

· Love does not think evil of others

· Love rejoices not in wrongdoing, but rejoices in the truth

· Love bears all things, believes all things, endures all things

· Love never fails

· Love is eternal

· Love is the greatest of all gifts

Paul learned well about love from the Great Psychologist! He built upon Jesus' principles, and gave us not only a model to strive for, but a guide to measure ourselves by. These characteristics are the way love is supposed to act, or behave itself. Love in this setting is a definite action-verb. Almost every Christian wedding has these beautiful words from

1 Corinthians 13 incorporated into the ceremony. I always invite couples to go back after a period of time has passed in their relationship and take a personal inventory of their life, asking the question, "It this the love I am giving to my mate?" The test is not how one is doing when things are going well—mountaintop experiences are usually easy—but rather how one is doing when things are in the valley. If we are faithful to these challenging words of love a year, five years, and ten years later in our relationship, it will change every word we utter, every deed we accomplish.

As you honestly measure how you love in comparison to this description from Paul, how are you doing in your relationships?

Demonstrating our love is a signal that we have heard the call of love and have clearly understood it. Love needs direction and, while it is highly important to love ourselves, we ultimately need to direct our love toward others. The deeds of love speak for themselves, and they stand above our spoken word. If there are no signs, or visible demonstrations of the love we claim to possess, one has a right to question the reality of that love. Jesus once cursed a fig tree! It looked as if it had fruit. The leaves were green, and Jesus approached it to find nourishment. When he got closer to the tree, there was no fruit to satisfy his hunger. It was barren! He felt deceived, and cursed the tree.[84]

Some of our lives are similar to the fig tree. Some of us look loving from a distance, but the closer others get to us, the more one discovers that our life is barren, we have no love to give. Our love will be judged not by the words on our lips, but by the actual fruits our love has produced.

There is such a lack of love in the world around us; a vacuum of horrendous dimensions. Look no further for the collapse of our society's morality. We have allowed love to be crowded out by our egos, greed, ambition, the desire for money, and personal profit. We are so careless with the precious gift of love.

The weeds of life have taken over our gardens of love!

We have such poor models of love given to us. It takes love for us to love. Many individuals are running on empty tanks, unable to give what they have not been given. Others feel cheated by love, and claim that they don't have love for their life's journey.

David was a fellow student of mine at Hope College; one of eight children from a devout religious family who lived outside of Holland, Michigan. His father was a successful farmer and business man. There was a sadness about David which was very obvious; emptiness which plagued him. This void was created by David's desire to believe that his father loved him.

David told me about his senior trip in high school, when his father took him to the airport. David wanted his father to put his arms around him and tell him, "Son, I love you!" Yet, not a single word was spoken. David told me this story several times, the tears streaming down his face. I was at a loss for words to console him. As I look back on our conversations, I can only hope that my listening to his story helped him. His experience taught me that love, regardless of how wonderful it is within the heart, if unexpressed and without direction, is incomplete.

What is the measurement of love in your life? Are you evolving into a more loving person? As we become more loving, we are becoming more Godlike. This is the challenge for our life. There is no higher goal worth attaining.

Questions to Ponder:

1. Who has given you unconditional love?
2. When have you been disappointed with the love you have received?
3. How do you show your love to others?

Psychological Insight

We are created for love, and there is no happiness we will find in life without love. As we mature in our personal lives, we will become more loving individuals. This is our supreme goal!

> *When a man abuses a woman,*
> *he only diminishes himself,*
> *for she is a child of God,*
> *and she is of his flesh.*

He Spoke As a Man to Men

*"There is, indeed one thing which
frightens me: the fear of God seems
to be dying out in the minds of men."
William Gladstone (1809 - 1898), speaking
to students*

Robert Pasick, a psychologist in Ann Arbor, Michigan, believes that men have been asleep for a long time, and they are just beginning to awaken. I also believe this awakening is long overdue. There are many myths about men, and unfortunately, men believe them! It begins early in childhood, when they are told "big boys don't cry." The myth continues with the rules that real men should be strong, independent, able to work out their own problems, and should not be vulnerable. Men should not let the competition see them sweat, and are taught to never show they are afraid. They are led to believe that thinking is more important than feeling, and certainly the business world rewards them for this. Perhaps, these myths contribute to the difficulty men have entering the office of a therapist when things go wrong in their relationships. Unfortunately, by the time they get there, it is often too late.

Another prevailing myth is that manhood is a status that is earned, and must continually be renewed by new demonstrations of courage. Thus, a man can be called a man one day, and a wimp the next, because he has failed to meet some artificial challenge society has set for him. Somehow, men are taught that life gives them a script that they must follow, and woe to them who do not.

Is it any wonder why men in our present society are confused about who they are, what they are suppose to think and feel, and especially, what is expected of them? A famous author appearing on a national talk show recently revealed that when he was growing up he was accepted as a jock by his friends. Then he decided he loved poetry. He felt he had to keep his new passion a secret from his peer group for fear of rejection. Now as a highly successful adult, he has had the opportunity to read his poetry to third graders, who think it is okay. However, when he reads the same poetry to ninth graders in New York City, the boys see it as a sign of being wimpy.

Sometimes women bring these same stereotypical expectations to relationships. In a session with me, Janice excitedly told me that she thought she had met the man of her dreams. He had a masculine side of him which she liked, yet he also had an insightful sensitivity which she also was attracted to. One day, during a session, she informed me that she had broken up with Greg. When I questioned her about her decision, I discovered her break-up was based on the fact that he showed her that he was vulnerable, and had expressed some self-doubts. Janice was disappointed by what she termed as "his lack of strength" and even went so far to call him "a wimp."

While I have heard only one side of the story, I can't help but wonder what Greg is thinking, and I can appreciate his confusion. Unfortunately, Janice is not unique in the double signal she is sending out to men.

It was my friend, Jim Russell, the director of Single Place at The First Presbyterian Church of Northville, Michigan, who urged to me to include some thoughts about what Jesus said to men in this book. At first, I felt confused about what this message might be. Jesus, I thought, never had a men's retreat where He pulled them aside and said, "Men, listen up! This is for you." However, the longer I thought about it; the more obvious it became: Jesus did have a message specifically for men. For over three years, Jesus and 12 men spent most of their time and energy together. This certainly qualifies for an intense seminar! They slept alongside of each other, ate together, shared ideas, sorrows and joys together. They laughed together and cried together. These men were in training, not only to be His disciples, but to be the best men possible.

Jesus taught by His example as well as by His word. He modeled what it was to be a man, and He certainly had specific ideas He shared with men.

What kind of man was He? For several months I pondered that question as I prepared this book. I studied the New Testament, and carefully reexamined the words and life of Jesus. I found that Jesus was a man's man. Men sought Him out, wanted to be in His company and desired to capture His insights. This only happens when other men feel that another man understands them and can relate to their problems and issues. Jesus met the criteria.

Another notable characteristic of Jesus was His courage. He was a courageous man. He stuck to his beliefs and risked His life to do so, and committed to truth no matter what. Jesus was downright gutsy. He had the courage of his convictions. He was not afraid to challenge the authorities for their faulty thinking and the enslavement of people. He often challenged the Jewish leaders, knowing it would ultimately mean death for Him. He knew that His entrance into the human arena would culminate in the sacrifice of His life. Frequently, Jesus warned and foretold of His death to His disciples.

Imagine if today you knew exactly how long you would live. Imagine if you knew how many years were left and you had it figured out to the day, the hour and the very minute. Imagine if you knew the exact way you would die and who would turn you in and what friends would walk away from your deathbed. You also knew you were going to face the terrible experiences of being betrayed, beaten, mocked and nailed to a wooden tree. How would you react, or more to the point, how would you survive living in the present? How would you make the days you had left meaningful and full, without having your attitude and work overshadowed by this "knowing." It is crystal clear to me as I read the narrative of His life that He had all of this information. More amazing is the fact that He functioned well, balancing Himself to stay on course to the very last breath of his life. This is beyond our comprehension. I just want to say—Wow!

Jesus was a man who openly loved people. Have you ever noticed how careful men are about showing love or saying those simple yet powerful words? "I love you." Apparently, they forgot to tell Jesus, "hide your love," or if they did, He ignored them.

One Gospel writer describes how when Jesus came to the grave of Lazarus, He wept because He loved him. Another time, a writer says when Jesus encountered the rich young ruler that he loved him. Instant love for another man—impossible! John, one of His disciples is known as the "disciple whom He loved." It is this same disciple who went on to write "God is love" and "Beloved let us love one another." John apparently listened well and learned from the Great Psychologist that love is the core of His message. Jesus motivated people because He loved them. Jesus inspired people because He loved them. Jesus drew people to Himself because they knew He loved them. As men living in today's confusing times, love is still the key to unlock life's doors, and especially the hearts of others.

As a man, Jesus took care of His earthly family. We do not know what happened to Joseph, His father, between the age of twelve when Jesus was found in the Temple and the age of thirty when He began His public ministry. It seems safe to assume that Joseph died a natural death. We do know that Jesus had a close relationship with His mother. There seemed to be a flow between them of mutual love and respect. She often traveled with Him and encouraged Him to perform the first miracle at Cana. Later, from the Cross, He asked His disciple, John, to care for her. How ironic where in our society a mother can raise four children, but four children cannot take care of one mother. This man, Jesus, was a good son!

I also believe that Jesus showed that men need to treat women with respect. Women loved Him. A group of women followed Jesus in His work and were constantly around Him. It says the twelve male companions were with Him, "as well as some women who had been cured of spirits and infirmities" (Luke 8:2-3). Four women are mentioned by name, one of them the wife of the steward of Herod. Then it states, many other women accompanied them. These women provided for His work out of their own finances. He was often found conversing with women, and He constantly sought out the company of Mary and Martha.

Throughout His stories, Jesus also has a word for men about being fathers. One of these truths comes from the story of the prodigal son. The young son of a wealthy father believed he had outgrown the small environment he was in, and decided to set out for greener pastures. The father allowed his son to go. How painful it must have been for him! Once the son left, the father never stopped looking down the winding road that led to the city in hopes of his son's eventual return.

In his son's pocket was all of his inheritance, which was soon squandered away on loose living. One day when the younger son had lost everything, he took a job feeding pigs. He was so hungry, he ate the pig's food! At that point, he realized it was better go home than to stay in his current situation.

Here is the best part of the story. Jesus says, [86]"But while he was still far off, his father saw him and filled with compassion; he ran and put his arms around him and kissed him."

The father saw him at a distance because he had a father's heart.[87] He never stopped looking down the road. He always had one eye on his work and one eye on the road. He had one eye on his wife and his older son, and one eye always on the road that took his son away. Perhaps he thought in his heart, "Someday I will see a tiny speck on that road, the form of my son, and I will see my son walking toward me instead of walking away from me."

And then that expectation became a reality. The prodigal son came home. The father granted his wayward son forgiveness, a magnificent welcome feast and accepted him back with great joy. This story not only has a message to fathers on how to deal with their children, but an insight on how our heavenly views us as His children.

Men who are not responsive to their children would be foreign to the thinking of Jesus. As a man, He would be shocked by men who avoid child support, seldom visit their children, or spend little quality time with them. Just as He said, "Render unto Caesar what is Caesar's and to God what is God's." I believe he would say "Render unto your children what is your children's." He would also be shocked at men who are side-stepping leadership in their homes. In the Jewish faith, it was the woman who stayed at home while the father attended the synagogue, learning the principles of the faith and interpreting them for the family. He was the spiritual leader, the priest within the home. The Jewish man did not leave it to the woman to do what God had appointed him to do.

This leads us to the therapeutic issue of responsibility. Responsibility is to take and do the tasks that are meant for you. It is to do the task that is yours, and uniquely yours. To not do it is to be irresponsible. Denial often springs from a lack of responsibility. If I ignore the problem, then I don't have to look at it, and I don't have to fix it. In my sessions with my clients, I have discovered that God created parents so we can have someone to blame!

Perhaps, this problem started in the garden when Adam blamed Eve for eating the fruit of the tree. Eve blamed the snake. Neither one of them would take responsibility for their actions. When Cain killed his brother and buried him in the earth, all he could say to God is, "Am I my brother's keeper?" Notice God never responded to that question. Perhaps God was saying, "Some questions are so ridiculous they don't need an answer." Are we to believe Cain did not know the answer?

And then there was Aaron, the brother of Moses; an excellent example of someone passing the buck. The greatest moment in the history of the Israelites was Moses receiving the Ten Commandments. Yet while Moses was on the mountain communing with God, the Israelites were in the valley denouncing the God who brought them out of slavery. Restless, they enticed Aaron to make for them a golden calf they could worship. What irony here, Moses is on the mountain top receiving the Ten Commandments, and in the valley the Israelites are creating a golden calf! Their greatest moment is also their lowest moment. Listen to how Aaron described the incident to his angry brother— they gave me their gold, [88]"and I threw it into the fire and out came this calf."

Aaron left a lot of details out. He conveniently forgot to tell his brother about all the artisans who worked several hours to mold the gold into the form of a golden calf. If you take Aaron's words at face value, you would be led to say "poor Aaron" and look what that nasty fire did, it made an image of idolatry. Israel may have come out of Egypt, but it took a long time for Egypt to come out of Israel. They suffered the consequences—God sent a plague on them for making a god of gold.

I am convinced that the healing process doesn't begin until the individual stops blaming others, their family backgrounds, and their present circumstances and take responsibility for their words and actions. Until that moment, they are wasting their time and energy. Taking responsibility may lead us to a difficult, painful time of self-examination, but it is necessary for positive change.

Much of my work is done in the area of domestic abuse. It is not unusual to see as many as eighteen individuals on probation. According to statistics, men are responsible for 95 percent of such abuse. Before my client comes in, I often get the opportunity to read the police reports describing the original incident which brought the individual in contact with the law. Regardless of the incident, the man usually always begins with these same words, "I don't need to be here," or "I didn't do it," or "She made me do it." To avoid the responsibility that belongs to us has become an inherent part of human nature. Jesus apparently knew this.

Consequently, the first giant step may be the most difficult. It comes with these words of realization, "I did it, I alone am responsible for my words and my actions!" That step puts our foot on the right path. There is no progress without taking responsibility.

Jesus hated hypocrisy of any kind. I define hypocrisy as being "two-faced;" one face you show at times, and a different face you show at other times. The purpose always appears to be the same: to impress others and have them think well of you. Everywhere Jesus went he saw hypocrisy and He was appalled by it. Jesus warned His disciples:

[89]"So whenever you give alms, do not sound the trumpet before you as the hypocrites do in the synagogues and in the streets, so that they may be praised by others."

[90]"And whenever you pray, do not be like the hypocrites; for they love to stand and pray in the synagogue and the street corners, so that they may be seen by others." [91]"And when you are praying, do not heap up empty phrases as the Gentiles do; for they think that they will heard because of their many words. Do not be like them."

[92]"And whenever you fast, do not look dismal, like the hypocrites, for they disfigure their faces to show others that they are fasting."

Another time He talked about the hypocrites who are quick to judge others for the speck in someone else's eye, while the person who judges has a log in his own eye. More than once Jesus warned against the false teachings of the Pharisees and Sadducees.

There are two important psychological principles at work in these passages: authenticity and honesty. In my thinking, there is a vast differences between these two virtues. Perhaps you have seen those decorative imported dolls made of wood. On the outside a figure of a doll is painted, and when you take the top off, there is an identical doll, only smaller, that appears inside. If you continue, there are usually several of these, each looking identical and each smaller. Authenticity, at least the ideal, is like that doll: what you see on the outside and what you get on the inside are the same. In other words, if you are kind and loving outwardly to others, it is what you truly are on the inside.

I always encourage persons to be authentic. Many people may not act like their true selves because of their insecurities and fears, rather than intentionally trying to be dishonest. Sometimes, because of their woundedness from earlier childhood experiences or other relationships, they are afraid to show themselves as they really are. They put their walls and barriers up. Walls to keep them within, and walls to keep others out. By doing so, they have decreased their vulnerability—so they think—but love by its very definition means vulnerability. Not being authentic is usually driven by feelings of fear.

Being honest in relationships is very different, because to be dishonest, one has to be intentional. Honesty is a significant ingredient we all desire in relationships. It is the pivotal point in all relationships. To be honest is to display truthfulness and integrity in my word and in my behavior. To men, it means that what I say is truth, and will be the truth in my life. What I say I will do. I will do nothing less, or take any action to discredit my truth. Honesty has become a rarity in our society. Jesus said the dishonest already have their rewards, they sit in the best places, men praise them for their offerings and their prayers. The greatest reward of all, the one God gives, is withheld from them. Dishonesty is usually driven by deceit.

Be authentic, be real in your relationships. Be who you are from within and show it outwardly. Be honest and let your word and your deed be your truth. Whatever you do, let it be pleasing to God. Remember that nothing is really a secret. God has not structured the universe for secrets.

Men, Jesus has a lot to say about children. Children are sacred gifts to us here on earth. They are His and only lent to us for only a brief moment of time. As I understand the message of the Great Psychologist, some truths are clothed in beautiful words and stories. There are other messages that are given more directly, with strong intensity; harsh words and even warnings. Jesus challenged His disciples with four thoughts about children: We must become humble as a little child, we must not cause them to stumble, we should not despise them, and as we treat children, we treat Him. These are sobering thoughts. Listen to His stern warning, "If anyone of you put a stumbling block before one of these little ones who believe in me, it would be better of you if a great millstone were fastened around your neck and you were drowned in the depths of the sea." Again He says, "Take care that you do not despise one of these little ones; for I tell you, in heaven their angels continually see the face of my Father in heaven." Don't mess with God's children!

One of the saddest stories that was told to me was about a little boy. The boy was only eight years old and was from a poor family. Every week he walked by himself to Sunday School at a nearby church. One day, a neighbor who didn't believe in this "God stuff" met him on the way home. The older man looked at the boy's worn shoes with his toes coming out of the front and ridiculed the boy, "If God loves you why doesn't he buy you a pair of shoes?" The young boy was stunned and at a loss for words, but only for a moment. Then he said, "God told someone to buy me a pair of shoes, but they forgot!" Oh, out of the mouth of babes!

It is obvious that the Great Psychologist will hold us accountable for how we treat children. Men—fathers—He is speaking to us.

The most difficult cases I have dealt with over the years are those which involve the abuse of children. A seventeen -year-old girl I counseled lived with her divorced mother, who was abusive and an alcoholic. Molly soon tired of mother's flow of boyfriends in and out of the house, and asked her father if she could come and live with him. He was reluctant. She pleaded with him. But, he was newly married and told her he needed time with his new wife. Finally, she was granted permission to be with her father.

Molly tried to get along with her new stepmother, but the stepmother was jealous of the time she and her father spent together. Then she noticed that her stepmother was poisoning her father's mind with things which were not true about her. She continued whispering negative things in his ear until it started to ruin the good relationship she shared with her father. Her father sided with his new wife.

The inevitable day came when Molly was told she had to leave. She was told she was "too much trouble," even though she was doing well at school, her room was always clean, and she helped around the house. Her stepmother helped her pack her bags in silence. Since she had nowhere to go, she was handed over to Social Services. Molly described how she sat on the front porch with her suitcase packed and her jacket on waiting for them to come. Her father and her stepmother were inside watching television. She felt crushed. As she told this story in my office, Molly did not only cry, she wept a river of tears. While I tried to be professional, a few tears of my own ran down my cheeks.

Over the years I have met many men in and out of therapy. In recent years, one of the interesting characteristics about my practice is that I now see twice as many men as I do women. This is, I believe, a sign of the awakening of men from their deep sleep of indifference. This is a new and exciting challenge for me, and I am savoring these moments of assisting in such a critical area. I am helping some men understand the void in their lives caused by the lack of the presence of a caring father. I am trying to humbly teach them what it means to be a man in a society where roles and expectations are confused.

Perhaps the new breed of man we need is epitomized by General Norman Schwartzkopf, the successful commander-in-chief in the Gulf War against Iraq. In an interview on national television with Barbara Walters, she was surprised that he became tearful when he talked about the importance of his family and his love for them. Barbara Walters questioned him about this show of emotion from such a leader of men. After all he was a man's man, a great example of a tough soldier to young soldiers. Then Schwartzkopf made the surprising statement that he did not trust a man who didn't cry. He was the chief of the army, yet he was vulnerable enough to show his emotions. This kind of man you can respect.

Jesus was man who knew what He believed, followed the truth, and was in touch with His feelings. He was not afraid to show His emotions and cried on more than one occasion. He wept at the loss of his friend Lazarus. He wept over Jerusalem. He respected women and enjoyed their company. He did not seek to control or abuse any other person He came in contact with. He was responsible for His words and deeds, and taught that others should be responsible as well. He taught that children are sacred gifts and, unless you have the humility they possess, you can not enter the Kingdom of God. Show them your love and approach them as your mission in life. Grant them unconditional love, and guide them and give them what they need in life, your time as well as your energy. Love your family and take care of your mother and father. Have integrity in your life. Be authentic and real in your relationships. Let your word be your truth and be honest with those around you. Hold fast to your truth and follow it with courage in your life.

These are the insights, Jesus, the Psychologist, has for men. If we are wise we will take His words at face value.

Questions to Ponder

1. What kind of relationship did you have with your father?
2. If you are a man, how would you rate yourself as a father? As a husband? As a man?
3. How do you treat the children in your life?

Psychological Insight

It is a big responsibility to be a man in the 21st century. Love those around you with an unconditional love and be sensitive to them. Let your behavior always be consistent with your words. Review the last paragraph of this chapter, and consider the challenges it offers any man courageous enough to follow Jesus.

Between us and heaven or hell there is only life, which is the frailest thing in the world.

—Blaise Pascal, Pensees' (1670)

He Said Forgiveness Must Be a Part of Your Life

"A relationship where there is no forgiveness has already died, the individuals involved may not know it, but it is ready for burial!"

Troy was traumatized by his divorce. He tried hard to save his marriage, but his wife, Melissa, had difficulty settling down. Even Sheila, their two-year-old daughter, did not seem to deter Melissa from going out with her friends to the local pub at least twice a week. Melissa was determined to "have fun and enjoy life."

Troy suspected all along that Melissa was not just having fun with the girls. He believed—correctly—that she was being unfaithful to their marriage vows. After five years of rocky marriage, Troy and Melissa's relationship ended in divorce.

To say that Troy is angry and unforgiving would be an understatement. He feels betrayed by Melissa. Unfortunately, this lack of forgiveness has hindered him from moving forward. He is still holding on to the past for dear life. He has had trouble forming new relationships because of his tremendous lack of trust in women. His anger is still driving him, and he is still focusing on the wrong that was done to him.

Jesus taught that forgiveness must be a part of one's relationships. Nothing will impact us more negatively than a lack of forgiveness. How important is forgiveness? It is mentioned at least twenty-four times in the gospels of Matthew, Mark, Luke, and John. Most of these references are direct quotes from Jesus sharing His truths about forgiveness. The biblical writers must have realized that it was a key ingredient to His message concerning life.

Jesus gives another great psychological insight that leads us not only to a balanced life, but for us to find our own forgiveness. Jesus' own forgiveness of His disciples, of those who crucified Him, as well as Simon Peter who denied Him three times, are all examples of His approach to forgiveness. His model of forgiveness shows us how He dealt with all He came in contact with, and how He treats us today. Jesus knew the power of forgiveness, as well as the toxic poison where there was a lack of forgiveness.

Jesus taught his disciples to pray the prayer to His Father and to include these words, [93]"And forgive us our debts, as we also have forgiven our debtors."

On another occasion, Peter came and asked Jesus if his brother wronged him, [94]"how often should I forgive? As many as seven times?" Jesus said to him, "Not seven times, but I tell you seventy-seven times."

The scariest principle Jesus teaches is that our forgiveness in life depends upon how we forgive others. He makes it clear we cannot ask from His Father what we have not given to others. And yet to be human is to desperately need forgiveness.

Joanne said she could not forgive her grandfather. She alleged that he had molested her when she was eight years old, and it had gone on for two years. The molestation usually happened when her mother would go shopping and she was suppose to be "in the safe custody of her grandfather." When he died, she was emotionally unable to go to the funeral. When she finally got up enough nerve to tell her mother the real reason she did not attend the funeral, her mother scolded her. She accused Joanne of trying to defame the good memory of her grandfather, especially since he was now unable to defend himself.

Joanne is in her thirties now, and having trouble with her present relationship. She blames part of it on the scars she received in her childhood. Through her tears, she has informed me she is not going to let "grandpa off the hook," and she "won't forgive that man." I'm paraphrasing— her words in my office were not that polite! I can still hear her voice and see the intensity of her look.

Forgiveness may be the hardest thing we do in life!

My father did not come to my wedding. Instead, he went out and got "totally drunk." I was angry with him about it for years, and I couldn't forgive him. "How could he ruin what was suppose to be my perfect day?" I reasoned. While my lack of forgiveness did not totally impair my relationship with him, I held on to that negative response for a long time while he was alive.

The Great Psychologist in his wisdom, however, taught me some new lessons about forgiveness. I would like to call this new learning "re-framing," or "seeing the same incident from a new perspective." My moment of enlightenment came after I had suffered my own tragedies in personal relationships and had to struggle to live through some sad endings and new beginnings. I also discovered that you don't have to believe in divorce to live through one. When these experiences impacted my life, I was able to look at my wedding day from my father's perspective and try to understand his feelings that particular day.

My mother was at my wedding with her new partner. After living in Tarrytown, New York, I was leaving the day after my wedding to head for Holland, Michigan, to attend my third year at Hope College. From there I would go on to Western Theological Seminary where I would be for another three years. My father and I had reconciled just two years earlier. Now I was leaving for good.

As I re-framed that original incident, I realized my moment of gain was his moment of loss. My day of happiness was really his day of sadness. No wonder he went out for a drink! I wasn't trying to excuse my father, but I was trying to understand what he must be feeling. Now instead of berating my father, I had compassion for him and the pain I believe he felt that day. I reasoned that it must have been difficult to see my mother, now remarried, and to realize that she had moved on with her life. I know he was still in love with her. It must have also been difficult to know that I was moving away from him after such a short reunion. As I gained insight into that day, I saw my father not as the strong parent, but as another human being with weaknesses like I possessed. When I walked in his shoes, and saw things from his perspective, the situation looked very different.

Perhaps what we don't realize about forgiveness is that it is under the umbrella of love. Forgiveness and love are not disconnected, but part of the same fabric. How we forgive is a barometer of how we love. If we love our neighbor as ourselves, if we pray for our enemies as we are encouraged to do, then forgiving them is easier. There is a paradox here, however. The more deeply we love someone, the more vulnerable we become and the deeper can be our hurt from some inconsiderate or selfish act.

Jesus must have felt this dilemma. He loved both Peter and Judas equally. Yet one denied him and came back for forgiveness; the other betrayed him and committed suicide. It is my belief that both could have had the same forgiveness. We will never know why Judas did not return and accept forgiveness from Jesus.

The supreme gift of forgiveness comes from Jesus, Ph.D. He has never asked us to do what He was not willing to do Himself. Think of the Cross! Imagine the long path Jesus took to get there; the struggle in the garden with the guards who came to capture Him; the trial before Pilate; the beating He took at the hands of the Romans and how they forced Him to carry His own weapon of destruction; and, finally, His crucifixion. As Jesus, Ph.D., hung from the Cross that day, He said, [95]"Father, forgive them, for they do not know what they do." Could you have uttered those words?

There is no greater forgiveness within our earthly life!

The Master Psychologist is clear. If we want forgiveness, we must give it. Once we receive it, we must continue to give it. We receive forgiveness in direct proportion to what we give.

I have often asked myself, "Why is forgiveness so hard for some individuals?" Here are two observations. The stronger one's self-esteem, the easier it is to forgive. The weaker one's self-esteem, the more difficult it is to forgive. It takes inner strength to forgive, and the stronger we are on the inside, the easier forgiveness can happen.

My second observation is that those with a strong support system also find it easier to forgive. When you get your support from other places, rather than one place (or person) you are stronger because not all of your eggs are in the same basket. If you only have one person who is your support person, and that is the person who betrays you, how traumatic! When you have support from many different sources, forgiveness seems to be easier.

Earlier in this chapter, we heard part of Joanne's story. Joanne went on to share in her sessions that her grandfather never admitted he had ever done anything wrong, and consequently never asked her for forgiveness. Her words were sharp and harsh. Joanne has had to learn that if we wait to forgive the other person until they deserve it, then it isn't forgiveness. The truth is that often those who want to be forgiven may never deserve it. Do it anyway! On the other hand, Joanne was guided to realize that her grandfather wasn't on the hook, she was. As long as she was unforgiving, she would stay hooked.

Forgiveness releases not only the person who is forgiven, but also the one doing the forgiving. It frees their heart from the poison of bitterness and anger. The unforgiving heart is usually angry, and anger always blocks the flow of love in our lives. Lack of forgiveness always builds walls; walls so high that love has difficulty getting over, but walls that keep love in. The unforgiving heart is captive to its own lack of forgiveness. Where there is forgiveness, there is freedom and the power of love. Where there is a lack of forgiveness, there is bondage.

There is one more insight about forgiveness I want to share with you. It comes from a friend of mine who lived through a very ugly divorce, and saw only too late that he should have responded to his wife earlier.

John discovered you don't have to believe in divorce to get one. One day, as John was beating himself up for the millionth time for the mistakes he made in the marriage, I leaned forward from my seat and whispered. "John, why don't you give to yourself what God has already given to you?" John stopped his self-absorbing behavior and became quiet. "And what is that?" he asked?"

"Forgiveness," I said. "Forgiveness!"

Why do we think we can accept the forgiveness of God and say "yes" to it without forgiving ourselves? We may find in life that it is easier to forgive others than to forgive ourselves.

There is nothing cheap about forgiveness. Jesus, Ph.D., knew this better than anyone. Forgiveness cost Him His life. Perhaps this is a key insight into forgiveness: it never happens without the person who does the forgiving giving part of himself.

Jesus teaches that an unforgiving heart is unforgivable. Forgiving and being forgiven are all part of the same truth. A man or woman who refuses to forgive cuts themselves off from the very love and mercy they need.

Questions to Ponder:

1. Who in your life haven't you forgiven?
2. Have you forgiven yourself for the things you have done wrong?
3. Have you accepted your humanness?

Psychological Insight

We need forgiveness in our daily lives. We need to accept our own imperfections. Forgiveness never ends. Forgiveness sets us free from toxic thoughts and negativism. As you forgive others, make room to forgive yourself.

He Accepted People Where They Were And Challenged Them

"Of all the things you will encounter in your life, the most powerful thing is your opportunity."

I met Mr. Abenshine, a teacher at Ottawa Hills High School, during my junior year. I wish now that I had met him sooner. With my parent's divorce and our sudden move from Poughkeepsie, New York, to Grand Rapids, Michigan, my grades plummeted during most of my years in high school. By the eleventh grade, I was beginning to wake up, but just a little.

Mr. Abenshine taught American history, a class I needed for graduation. To be candid, I wasn't really excited about the class, and I figured I was sure to do my usual "C" or "D" work. After the second day of class, he asked me to stay afterward. I was surprised to be singled out. When everyone had left the classroom, he turned and said to me with a smile, "Tom, there is no reason why you can't get an 'A' in my class." Stunned, I looked around to make sure he was talking to me.

"There isn't?" I stammered back.

"Absolutely no reason," he said confidently.

I walked away wondering what he knew that I didn't.

I hardly knew this teacher, and he couldn't know that much about me. However, from that day a strange phenomenon began. I found myself reading my history assignments with greater interest and studying harder for his class, than any other. With this new approach, I was discovering that I was liking history—a revelation for me.

The semester went by quickly. One day after the final exam, Mr. Abenshine was in class surrounded by at least a dozen students asking for their final grades. When it was my turn, he said, "Bruno, *A* " I was so surprised I asked him again, and this time he put a ruler under my name and followed it to the end of the ledger. Again, he said " *A!*"

"An *A* ?" I questioned, in amazement.

"Well, if you don't want an *A*, we can change it and give it to someone else," he said as he winked at me.

"No, no," I said, as I gleefully walked away.

After that I received an *A* in every class I took from Mr. Abenshine.

As I look back, I realize now that he taught more than history. Mr. Abenshine knew a lot about psychology and he loved his students. I "aced" every class I took from him and started using the tools I learned from that experience in other courses. Most of all, I came to realize that he believed in me before I believed in myself. Perhaps he learned this principle from the Master Psychologist!

Jesus accepted people for themselves. In Scripture we read that as Jesus went about His ministry, He left Judea and started back to Galilee. To do so, He had to go through Samaria. What happened next shows us that Jesus was willing to break ranks, push the envelope, and move beyond contemporary prejudices. Near the town of Sychar, there was a well which was famous because the patriarch Jacob once used it.

Jesus was tired from His trip, and He was drawn to the well because He was thirsty. But He did not have anything with Him to draw the water. A woman of Samaria came to draw water at this same time. He asked the woman for a drink. The woman was surprised by the request of Jesus, and said, [96] "How is it that you, a Jew, ask a drink of me, a woman of Samaria?" She was referring to the fact that there were ill feelings between the Samaritans and the Jews. These ill feelings were generated over the issue of where they should worship.

The two boundaries Jesus crossed were: speaking to a Samaritan woman in public, and talking to someone the Jews considered the enemy. Jesus, Ph.D., did this without hesitation or reservation. As they talked, Jesus asked her to go and call her husband. She admitted to Him that she was not married. Jesus revealed to her that He already knew that the present man she was living with was not her husband. She was amazed by His knowledge of her personal life, and by the time the conversation ended He had also revealed to her that He was the Messiah who was coming into the world.

When the disciples came back from buying food in town, it is recorded that they [97]"were astonished that he was speaking with a woman, but no one said "What do you want?" or "Why are you speaking to her?"

The surprises go on, especially when this woman runs into town to tell her neighbors about this encounter with this stranger. [98]"Come and see a man who told me everything I have ever done! He cannot be the Messiah, can he?"

With all that Jesus knew about this woman, about her past and her present situation, we should note that Jesus had no prejudice towards her, no judgment, no ultimate condemnation. This woman had a lot to hide, but He accepted her! He accepted her where she was and what she was at that moment. She responded positively to this Master of human behavior and was drawn to him. As she ran into the village, she invited friends and strangers not to come and see a man who knew everything she had done and condemned her, but a man in whose presence she felt acceptance. She questioned them, "Could He be the One we have waited for?"

Word of mouth is still the best advertisement for any good psychologist. Jesus accepts us the same way He accepted this woman of ancient Samaria, and we should accept others in the same way. Isn't this one of our greatest desires, to be accepted, which translates into being loved? My friend, Dr. Robert Schuller, says man greatest need is to be respected. This also translates into being accepted and loved. Jesus granted to this woman what she so desperately needed.

Another time when Jesus entered Jericho, and a crowd had gathered, He came upon a man whom we might say was "vertically challenged." Zacchaeus was short! To see Jesus, he climbed into a tree, which put him above the crowd.

As the crowd moved on and Jesus came to him, He did something that is not recorded anywhere else in the Word; He invited Himself to someone's house without being asked. Zacchaeus was one of the most unlikely candidates for a visit from a spiritual leader of great popular appeal. Zacchaeus was the chief tax collector of that particular area, and was despised and looked down by those around him. In fact, the crowd grumbled when Jesus went into his house.

But when Zacchaeus came away from his encounter with Jesus, everything changed. He said, [99]"Look, half of my possessions, Lord, I will give to the poor, and if I have defrauded anyone of anything, I will pay back four times as much."

What in the world could this master of human behavior have said to Zacchaeus during those brief moments? Whatever He said, it motivated Zacchaeus to surprising and beautiful acts.

But Jesus didn't stop there. In one of His most famous encounters, a woman caught in the act of adultery was brought to Jesus by the temple leaders. They hoped they could trap Him. Jesus invited those who were without sin to cast the first stone. Slowly the leaders and crowd put down their weapons and slunk away. When the crowd had gone, just two people were left, Jesus and the woman, He turned and said to her, [100]"Neither do I condemn you."

Jesus marched to a different drummer. Some applauded Him for it, while others despised Him. In each incident, not only did Jesus accept people where they were in life and show that He was colorblind and gender blind, but He challenged each person to take their life to a higher level.

His challenge to the woman at the well was, [101]"those who drink of the water that I give them will never thirsty … The water that I give will become … a spring of water gushing up to eternal life."

To Zacchaeus, the challenge that Jesus gave was to become a part of His kingdom. And when he accepted that invitation and responded positively, Jesus said, "Salvation has come to your house this day."

To the adulterous woman He said, [102]"Neither do I condemn you, Go and sin no more."

The invitation to have a new beginning is still open to you and me. What a great psychological principle for us to embrace in our lives!   You don't need to try to be something you are not. You don't need to hide your past and come in shame. You can be yourself with all of your imperfections.

Jennifer leaned forward from the green couch she was sitting on in my office. It was her second visit. She appeared to be nervous. "I hope you still like me when you get to know me," she said.   I knew what she meant! I'd felt that way myself.

I smiled at her, a warm, accepting smile that let her know she was okay and in the right place. That was a year ago. I have since heard all the secrets she was afraid of sharing and couldn't even admit to herself. I still like her!

If we can be accepted at our worst, certainly we can be accepted at our best.   The challenge of the Master Psychologist is timeless: "You can do better, start now and do it!"

Questions to Ponder:

1. Are you stuck where you are? Do you need a new start?
2. Are you colorblind and gender blind in your relationships with others?
3. Are you accepting the persons in your life where they are or are you making them live up to your expectations?

Psychological Insight

You are accepted for whom you are! Wherever you find yourself, and at whatever age, you can have a new beginning—right now. It is Jesus' gift to you!

Give the gift to yourself.

> *"The truth will set you free,*
> *but first it will make you miserable."*
> —James A. Garfield

He Sought Truth And Freedom

"Therapy, in one way or another, is finding out the truth about you!"

Kelly and Andy's marriage was in serious difficulty, and my office was their last stop before a divorce. Kelly initiated the sessions, driven by her own feelings of unhappiness in the relationship. Andy said, aside from a few glitches, he thought the relationship was okay. After ten years of marriage, he stated he didn't share her unhappiness and felt their ups and downs were normal.

Andy was vague about what he thought might be wrong in the relationship. Kelly shared that she was not getting the love she wanted out of the relationship and was often left hanging about his feelings towards her. In one of the sessions, she confronted Andy and simply asked him, "Do you still love me?" His rely was "Well, after ten years, I'm still here."

I began on the last joint session by asking each one of them to think about what responsibility they would accept for what was not working in the marriage. Kelly thought she had become too sensitive, and since she had gained weight, needed more compliments that she was okay. She reasoned that perhaps she was too needy. When Andy was asked the same question, he responded by saying "She must think I am doing something wrong, because we're in your office." Andy didn't think he was doing anything wrong and if he was, he didn't know what it was.

At the end of the last session, it was obvious that Andy was reluctant to come back. When I asked why, he said that he wasn't sure the therapy was working, and it cost too much money. Kelly was willing to come back, which she did for the next few months. She said persistently in her sessions that she wasn't feeling loved by him. "Something changed about two years ago in the marriage but I can't pinpoint exactly what it is," she said. She simply concluded that Andy's feelings had changed.

Something didn't feel right. I could identify with Kelly feeling left up in the air, because, I realized that is the way I felt after their sessions. I discovered I was bothered by Andy's vagueness and came to the conclusion that his vagueness about what he really felt or believed was a camouflage. While I believed that she loved him and she verbally expressed that, I did not feel the same warmth and passion toward her from Andy. I noticed that at the end of the session, when she tried to hug and kiss him he would physically pull away. His non-verbal communication was clear.

Kelly and Andy eventually separated. Kelly was devastated by the experience, but Andy was vague about it. He never admitted there was anyone else in the picture, but the person Kelly suspected he might be having an affair.

So for two years, Andy was vague so he could hide the truth from Kelly—he didn't love her anymore and there was someone else. This is why he didn't respond to her as he had earlier in the marriage. It is possible that Andy was not only hiding this truth from her but also himself. However, the counseling only made him less considerate and less loving than before.

Time had cut through the vagueness and revealed the truth. It's tough to fake being in love. While Andy was vague about getting a divorce, Kelly said she could not live in a loveless marriage. However, Andy is now getting what he probably wanted all the time.

Jesus had a lot to say about truth, and especially freedom. These two concepts are joined together in the same chapter, because I believe they are inter-linked. Truth is always liberating and moves us toward freedom. Freedom, on the other hand, should always be used to move us toward truth.

Jesus was dedicated to truth. Freedom is a wonderful dividend that naturally follows truth. He said to his disciples, "I am the way, the truth, and the life."[103] Later, during His trial before the Roman officials that led to His crucifixion, He declared, [104]"Everyone who belongs to the truth listens to my voice," Those who knew the truth were able to recognize it in Him. The same principle is at work today.

It was Pilate who asked Jesus, [105]"What is truth?" He asked at a time when the truth was clouded, and there was much confusion. Jesus stood before him accused by the religious leaders of being "King of the Jews," thus an enemy of the state. Pilate wonders if He really is a King, and worthy of death. According to Rome there can only be one Emperor and one King. Pilate sought to know the truth! Jesus makes it clear that He is a King, and for this truth He has come into the world. However, if He was here to set up a physical kingdom his followers would have taken arms and fought for Him. His Kingdom will rule the hearts and minds of men and women. It is in this moment in history that Pilate asks his eternal question, [106]"What is truth?" Whether he ever totally understood what Jesus was saying to him is not clear.

Truth expands, yet it never changes. It is constant and eternal. What was true yesterday is still true today. There is truth outside of us as well as within us. There is eternal truth outside of us that can be accepted as reality. As we internalize what we hold to be truth, it becomes our truth and our reality. Thus we can say, "This I know or this I believe!" However, when we compromise with truth, or accept half-truths, we move towards contamination, and the possibility of illness, an illness that can lead to our spiritual and psychological death. When we are dedicated to truth in our lives, we may not live with less problems, but we certainly have less things to cover and hide. This will help to make our life less complicated.

We need to strive to see the world and our lives as God sees it. This would be the ultimate truth. Faith is an effort to move in that direction. This is why the Great Psychologist said, " I am the way, the truth, and the life." He is the embodiment of truth. He would always have us move toward truth and keep truth as a priority. As we live and walk in truth we will have less consequences to pay in life. He knew that the psychological dividends to our health would be great.

In general, the tabloids and newspapers are doing more than reporting the news. They report what others thought could be kept as a secret. The sickness of our present society is the unspoken belief that truth doesn't always have to be told and we can hide it. The sickness of our society is that the justice system at times is no longer dedicated to truth, but who has the best lawyer and what legal technicalities the guilty can use and avoid punishment. Big businesses often do what is profitable rather than what is in the best interest of the public. The Great Psychologist says there are no secrets—there is only truth, the truth about God, the truth about Him and the truth about ourselves. Regardless of what we hide and conceal in life, we cannot deny the truth. In the end, truth always emerges and always wins.

In therapy, truth may be painful. Usually a person who is trapped in addiction will avoid the truth at all costs. Denial is always the enemy of truth and freedom. If one denies a problem, then there is nothing to solve or fix. It may keep a person in their comfort zone, but it is a false comfort zone.

In 1967, I found myself in the office of a psychiatrist. My unsolved issues from my childhood had finally caught up with me, and even though those around me saw me as successful I knew I was struggling within. My parish work was fruitful, but I was granted a sabbatical to heal. My sessions with the psychiatrist was short, only thirty minutes a week, twice a week. The psychiatrist was very blunt, pulled no punches and was straightforward. He did emotional surgery on me—a painful process! By this, I mean he helped cut away from my life what we call dysfunctional and unhealthy. One of the startling things he told me was that I was a negative and pessimistic person. Not only didn't I agree with him, but I was insulted. However, it took some deep introspection before I realized I was in denial, and stuck in my pride.

I found that his very direct interventions were helpful to me, and I was at a time in my life where I was ready for it. He explained a phenomenon I have discovered at work in many individual lives. I acted positive and spoke positive, but in the inner recesses of my heart where I really operated from, I was negative, not really believing "things would work out for me." I did believe they would work out for other people, but not for me. So in spite of my many successes, my head had not caught up to where my body was. My head was still living in the ghetto of poverty and failure while my body was surrounded by the trappings of success. There was a sharp division between my head and my heart. All such dichotomies lead to being unhealthy, spiritually and psychologically.

As I examined my life, I discovered the truth. I was constantly replaying my failures, and operating from those failures, believing they were the laws that governed my life. Unfortunately, I had a lot of failures to prove my point. And when individuals accept this agenda, they eject the positive anyway because it doesn't compute. This is like telling a young man he is handsome, and deep within he doesn't really believe you. He believes you have an ulterior motive for this positive message.

Therapy is a discovery of the truth for your life. A person's reality is usually their truth. Your reality is what you have accepted as truth in your life. In that sense, perhaps therapy is an attempt to modify and change one's reality, consequently changing the truth as one sees it. One has a right to expect a therapist to be truthful and have integrity. If one is going to make any progress in therapy, the one who seeks to be healed must also be truthful. Progress will depend on being gut-wrenchingly honest. Too many have come in asking therapists to help and guide them, but to also guess what is wrong with them.

Truth is a well-kept secret in our modern society. What is it that makes us run from the truth? What is it that makes us hide from that which can set us free?

Dishonesty or "untruth" always leads us to dysfunction. One of the dysfunctional aspects of unhealthy families is the need to keep secrets. John Bradshaw said that what we don't know can hurt us. Where there is a need for secrets, it is usually because we are trying to cover what desperately needs to be in the light. It is the dysfunctional family that tries to keep secrets, which is usually an attempt to protect what one is doing wrong and continuing doing it.

Kathy was an incest victim I counseled who was repeatedly told by her father as a twelve-year-old child not to tell anyone he was sneaking into her bedroom late at night and fondling her. "Don't tell your mother, or any of your friends, either." In short, keep it a secret.

This secrecy allowed the father to continue for years in his selfish, damaging, behavior towards his daughter. Because of the "don't tell" attitude, it also kept Kathy from discovering that this was not normal and consequently should not be happening. She assumed that it was probably also occurring to her girlfriends, but no one was suppose to talk about it. Thus, she came to accept this tragic behavior for her life as "normal," even though she detested it.

Individuals coming from this same frame of mind, "the keeping of family secrets," usually find therapy difficult. They feel that they are betraying the family when they talk about their family's dysfunction, or reveal the dirty family secrets. They are ridden by guilt believing that they are doing something wrong. Often they state, "if my father and mother knew I was talking about this, they would be angry." Thus no healing can come to the dysfunction or the secrets. They are usually confused about boundaries and what is healthy and what is unhealthy. They believe they are being disloyal to their family by talking about them, thus they never see their family of origin objectively. However, there is no real psychological wellness without truth in one's life.

When Connie first came to me, she admitted that she was not being truthful in her relationship with her husband. However, she wanted to keep what she had done a secret. Then one day her husband came to her studio unannounced, and found her and her lover engaged in a romantic embrace. Her world came crashing in around her. Her secret was out!

After a stormy week, Connie and her husband, David, ended up in my office. Surprisingly, David asked her to stay and work on the marriage. Connie agreed to do so. However, what bothered me was that the man Connie was having an affair with was a friend of David's. David naively did not mind his wife continuing talking to him, but wanted all sexual relationships with him to stop. Connie promised to abide by this agreement, but she did not give up her friendship or contact with him.

Red flags were everywhere. Common sense tells us that reconciliation never works between three people: two is the right number! In her private session, I shared again my anxiety about any contact with Kevin. She insisted everything was fine. Two weeks later, she shared that they were sexually involved again. She also shared with me her guilt and her determination that she did not want this to happen.

She was surprised when I told her that she did want it to happen. I believe the principle of "intentionality" was working here. The law of "intentionality" is that what we intend (desire) to have happen, either consciously or unconsciously, we help made it happen. For example, if you wake up on a Sunday morning and say you are going to church, but deep within you, you do not want to go, that is your real "intentionality." Consequently, you may take your time drinking your coffee, or getting your shower. Time slips away, and suddenly you say, "Oh, my, it is too late to get to church on time."

The truth is that you didn't want to go in the first place and that is your real intention.

Back to Connie. One part of her admitted that her involvement with a man outside of her marriage was wrong, and she wanted to stop. Emotionally, however, she wanted to be involved, and that part of her was giving her new lover the green light. There was something within that new relationship that was satisfying her unfulfilled needs. The truth is that she might not end up with either person.

The saga of Connie and David is still being played out, but their relationship improved when they both realized that they must be ruthlessly honest with each other. When she recommitted to the marriage, their relationship took a giant step forward, but trust takes years to build and only one day to be destroyed. The outcome of their marriage is still pending.

Sometimes in our life we may all need to do a reality check, to check our truth with another individual's truth. A middle-aged attractive woman came in for a session and revealed to me that she had been accused of being flirtatious. Men were constantly coming on to her, and while this was ego-boosting at times, it was more often a nuisance. I asked if she thought she was a flirt. "I'm not sure" was her answer.

I gave her an assignment to ask at least four people whose opinions she trusted whether or not they thought she was flirtatious. I told her not to ask friends, but to ask people who would be objective and would give a truthful answer. When she came back she informed me that three of the people she asked thought she was flirtatious. She was somewhat surprised by this reality check. I told her that if others saw her as flirtatious, she had to take their opinion into account.

From there she worked on what signals she was sending out to others, women as well as men. She also had to work out what signals were innocent, but being misread by others. As she dug in to do her work, she admitted that the perception of her friends was not one she wanted to ignore. In the end she did a good job modifying and changing her behavior.

If we are wise we will be aware of how others perceive us. Their reality may hold truth for us that we need to look at. Life has a way of intervening in our life with its own reality. The wise person will weigh both realities and balance them.

It is not enough to talk about truth in our lives, it must be clear we are committed to it. As we do, we need to realize that truth is very significant to the teachings of the Great Psychologist. There are no secrets in the universe, there is only truth, and sooner or later that truth will be revealed. Where there is truth, there is light; where there is light, there is freedom; and where all of these are present, there is wholeness, which we need for our lives.

Where there is such truth, there is His presence and His healing touch!

Questions to Ponder:

1. How would you define truth?

2. What do you need to be more honest about in your life?

3. Is there too much freedom in your life, or not enough?

Psychological Insight

Therapy doesn't begin until you are truthful with yourself. Dishonesty of any kind always leads to dysfunction. Be truthful with all people in all relationships, for freedom will quickly follow behind. Where there is truth—there is the Great Psychologist and His kingdom of freedom.

He Was in Contact with the Highest Power

"To live is nothing, unless to live be to know Him by whom we live."
—John Ruskin, 1819-1900

The story is told of a woman who lived in upper state New York who constantly complained about her health problems. After going to several doctors, she ended up having a pill for every situation and almost every person in her life. She had a pill for stress, as well a pill to help her cope with her son-in-law, daughter-in-law, grandchildren, etc. It wasn't long before the window sill over her sink in the kitchen had a long row of medicine bottles. Soon word got around, and she was labeled by many friends and professionals as a hypochondriac.

One day she went to a doctor, who unbeknownst to her, knew of her reputation. The doctor politely listened to her latest ailment, and then she prepared herself for more sympathy and a new prescription. Instead, the doctor told her something she had not been told before. "I want you to drive to Niagara Falls and then I want you to stand at the edge of the water and..." Before he could finish, projecting what she thought he was going to say next, she blurted out, "I bet you want me to jump?" The doctor hesitated in his response and then said, "No, but I do want you to see something higher than yourself."

The woman, indignant, left in a huff, no doubt to get home to take a high blood-pressure pill.

Jesus not only believed in a higher power, He believed in the Highest Power of the universe. What did He say about the Highest Power? He believed that the highest power was His Father in heaven. Yes, He called Him Father! He kept in constant contact with His Highest Power throughout His earthly walk. He taught His disciples to do the same. He claimed that He had come from the Highest Power, His Father, to step into the human arena for a mission that would change history. After He completed His mission, He claimed He was going back to the Highest Power and be restored to His own power and glory.

Every 12 Step Program begins with a belief in a Higher Power. Why? Because it is the best place to begin. The beginning of the healing process has to be begin with a belief that something is greater than you, that Someone is greater than you. That "Someone" is apparently the foundation of your support system. The higher power as used in the 12 Step Program appears to have a double meaning.

First, it recognizes that there is the higher power within you. Within each one of us, there exists side by side the negative side of our personality as well as the positive. Perhaps, we could call this our lower side, or the dark side of our personality. It is ruled by earthly appetites and unruly drives, prejudices, etc. If we let this side of us run wild, it can easily get out of control. The other side of an individual is his or her good positive side that focuses on the lofty, divine, things of life. This side taps into our Higher Power, or the best of what is within you. It is your untapped potential that is there to be used, but you have to unleash it. This power, carnal, or divine is within you. It is the best of you, it is the worst of you.

The Higher Power within you is the best of you, it is your greatest potential waiting to be lived, it is your dreams still waiting to be fulfilled, it is finding the divine that is within you: for God has planted the divine spark inside of all of us.

It is your choice to decide whether the higher part or the lower part ultimately gets center stage. It is your choice to decide whether the best or worst of you dominates your thoughts and actions. Unfortunately, sometimes neither happens and we settle for mediocrity, and a life that is uneventful.

There is an entity that is the Highest Power that is separate from our being. God has an existence separate from us and outside of us. It is this belief in the Higher Power that is divine, or God as you define God. How you define God will determine whether He or She can help you.

Unfortunately, to many, God—the Highest Power— is a vague entity with little or no personality. Thus God is devoid of a real interest in our world or our plight. I have noticed that those who think of God in such vague terms and definitions as "a supreme intelligence up there," do not have a God that enters into their life in any meaningful way to help them. To the degree that their concept of Him is vague, so is their concept of a God who can intervene and guide them in their daily lives. When we look at how the Great Psychologist viewed God—the Highest Power—we can build a dynamic support system in our own lives.

What did the Great Psychologist say and believe about the Highest Power of the universe? Jesus did not have any vague concept about God. The Highest Power was not devoid of personality and was not just an intelligent source or power that had simply created the universe and let it go its own way. Nor did Jesus believe that after God created the universe He stepped back and forgot about it. First, He called the highest power, Father. Jesus saw God as a loving parent. There are some who call God a He or She. God is the perfect parent, and while He has been portrayed as a Father, it is my belief that as a perfect and whole parent, He does incorporate all that is feminine and all that is masculine into His being. He is the sum total of both.

The Highest Power, God the Father, is a loving Father, one who gives to His children what they need and cares of them. Jesus constantly makes this truth clear. He talked about the loving Father in the story of the prodigal son. He asked which one of us as a father would give our child a serpent when he asked for bread. Despite all our personal experiences with our parents here on earth, there is a compassionate Father who always loves us and listens to us.

The New Testament is written in Greek, but Jesus spoke in Aramaic. We now know that the words Jesus used to converse with His Father were not formal words of address. Scholars believe that Jesus used very informal language. Believe it or not, Jesus addressed His heavenly Father as Dad, or, Daddy! While this may seem unusual to us, it suggests a high level of intimacy, of understanding and closeness, between Father and Son. Jesus said, [107]"I and My Father are One." Because of this high degree of intimacy between them, He thought it was appropriate to address His father as "dada" or "daddy." This is an amazing insight in understanding the depth of their relationship.

Jesus once declared that no one knows the Son except the Father, and no one knows the Father except the Son. The knowing of which Jesus is sharing is at the highest and deepest divine level, which is beyond human comprehension. It is between God the Father and God the Son. Suffice it to be said, that it is an intimate, perfect, relationship of understanding and knowing that is at its deepest level.

Jesus was guided by the power of his Father. He claimed that what He personally was doing here on the earth, is what He saw is Father doing. He made this statement more than once. The power and authority He exercised here on earth, was authority given to Him by His Father, for all authority was given to Him.

He was in constant contact with His Father, clearly doing nothing without the knowledge and acceptance of His Father. We might be tempted to call this prayer, for it was, and in the life of Jesus it appears to be a running, continuous, conversation with His Father that never ended. This conversation was without limitations and was never limited to time or space. Such conversation could happen anytime, anywhere, under any circumstance and usually did. The flow of communication was powerful, dynamic, life changing, a merging of ideas, thoughts, and feelings that created a oneness in purpose and essence. Obviously, there is a mysterious part of this that we must let stand and accept, because it is beyond us. From this perspective, it is clear that Jesus would not make a move without informing and asking His Father.

How different this is from the way many of us live our lives! When faced with a crisis these words are often heard, "Well, there is nothing left to do but pray!" What an insult to the power of prayer. Prayer directed to God is the last thing we do, prayer is the first thing Jesus did.

There are some who may skip this chapter, thus missing the significance of understanding the benefits that comes from being rooted in a deep belief in the Highest Power. Our belief in the Highest Power of the universe is the foundation of our help. It is the core of everything that will happen to us, and the understanding we will gain from what has happened to us. It is the heart of our belief system, and it grounds us in the deep soil of believing the world in which we find ourselves is not one giant orphanage of doomed existence, but a temporary existence where we can be filled with love from our Father, who cares about our daily bread. Jesus taught His disciples to begin their conversation with God, with "Our Father."

He also stated that His Father has prepared a place for those who believe in Him. He said there are "many mansions," or many rooms there, and He personally would go there first and prepare a place for us to be with Him. The Great Psychologist promised our eternity would be spent with Him.

In His relationship with His Father He taught that help in available now. Right now!

Jesus shows us that Highest Power is the foundation of His life. Countless individuals everyday may gain psychological healing without relying or believing in God, but it is not what the Great Psychologist wants for us. It is the formula that worked for Him and one He believes will work for us. Believing in God as Our Highest Power is to call forth of all the best within us, our greatest possibilities and potential waiting to be expressed.   Without such a belief, we will never fully understand who we are, why we are here and where we are headed. Our total knowledge of the universe we live in will be limited.

There is a mythical legend that says man constantly abused the divinity that God granted to him. Then God took it and placed it within man, thinking it would be the last place he would look. Man has been searching for the Highest Power of his life ever since.

Questions To Ponder:

1. Describe in a few words what you think your Higher Power is?

2. What is the best in you that you would like others to know?

3. How many times during the day are in contact with your Highest Power?

Psychological Insight

Begin your psychological journey with recognizing the Higher Power within you. The Divine Spark which God has planted is within you. Be in contact often with the Highest Power, for He grants strength and guidance for the journey.

He Knew How to Listen

"How can there be communication if no one listens?"

One of the most frequent questions I am constantly asked is, "Why do couples break up?" Since I have been speaking to couples since 1965, I have developed some definite ideas. Very few couples break up because of too little sex or too much—this can be adapted to if they love each other. Couples do break up because of infidelity and lack of commitment.

Money appears to be one of the biggest issues that couples fight about the most. Too little money or poor money management puts tremendous stress on any relationship. This issue alone is responsible for leaving behind an enormous junk pile of broken relationships.

When love has died in any relationship, the relationship is in great crisis. If forgiveness is absent, the relationship will also be in crisis. Numerous individuals have shared with me over the years the absolute frustration of their mate's refusal to forgive within the relationship. Hopefully where there is great love, there will be forgiveness of equal measure. Without love and forgiveness, more than a red flag needs to go up. An SOS flare would be better!

One of the major causes of breakdowns in relationships is communication. Numerous relationships start out with good communication, or a healthy dialogue, but unfortunately end up in a monologue.

Jesus knew how to listen! There is no question in my mind that He did this well, and this is one of many reasons people He encountered responded to Him so positively. The purpose of listening is to bring the level of communication to its highest level—understanding. The dividend we gain is the intimacy which can come from such moments. We often think of intimacy as sexual involvement, but intimacy can exist between any individuals who seek to share their thoughts, ideas, their hearts and themselves. Hopefully, we will have this intimacy with several individuals throughout our lives.

A husband and wife, troubled by their relationship and lack of communication, came to see me for the first time. The husband was sitting on the edge of his seat, and did not seem to be attentive to his spouse speaking. In fact, it seemed that he couldn't wait for her to stop speaking. After his wife finished, I asked him if he knew what he was going to say before she stopped talking. "Yes," he eagerly replied. "Then you probably were not listening to her," I snapped. "Listen to her, until her very last word, then figure out what you are going to say," I continued. While he was not happy with the criticism, in the long run he admitted it was helpful.

There is very little listening going on in our society!

I've found that there are five stages that couples undergo in regard to communication:

· **The first stage is the courtship stage.** In this stage, communication is at its height. There is a great deal of verbal communication while each of the individuals are fascinated with each other and still discovering each other. The strength of this stage is that the individuals talk and share their feelings. Non-verbal communication is at its highest level as well. The couple at this time in their relationship are very aware of the needs of their mates and make great efforts to meet them.

· **The second stage of communication is the settling-in stage.** The honeymoon is over, and the real dynamics of the relationship emerges. This is still a good time for the couple. However, the intensity of communication which existed in the first part of their relationship has waned. The communication patterns that emerge out of the period of the relationship will set the stage for the rest of the relationship. It is not usually in this stage that the relationship runs into its greatest difficulty.

· **The third stage is one of coexistence.** In this stage, there is a shift of focus from each other to what they need to do to make the relationship work financially. There may also be a shift towards the pursuing of personal careers, interests or hobbies. The chase is over, consequently, they now concentrate on the stability and security of the relationship. There are usually two kinds of communication in this stage. One is shared information or facts, and the other deeper level is the sharing of feelings.

At this point in the relationship, let's change these words to content vs. process. Content is information about what I am doing; process is sharing how I feel about what I am doing. If I tell you I am going to work at 10 A.M., that is content. If I tell you I don't feel like going to work altogether, that is process. The difficulty with relationships

Jesus Ph.D.

in terms of communication is that throughout the five stages there is usually a shift from process toward content, until the moment when there is more content than process.

The business of schedules here becomes a great challenge to the quality of time that the couple spends together. In the third stage there is less dialogue and more monologue, as well as a shift towards content or information rather than authenticity of feelings.

· **The fourth stage is the confrontation stage.** In this stage one or both of the individuals in the relationship may come to the conclusion that their needs are not getting met. This may cause anger, vulnerability and frustration. During this time, one or both of the individuals may confront the other in verbal confrontation. This is a critical time because it may be a "bail out time" or "stay and work it out" time. However, there is another option that couples often take, and this is to divorce themselves from each other, emotionally and psychologically and stay in the "marriage." Obviously, this is a painful option and surprisingly, many couples end up in this painful stalemate. If one does stay and work on the communication it allows the couple to move to one of the most significant stages of the relationship—the time of co-creation.

· **The fifth and final stage is the co-creation stage** of the relationship, and the communication within it. This is a mature period for the couple when they realize that their mate cannot met all of their needs—and that's okay. They also realize that there is a high need to communicate "process" as well as "content" and this is a priority. Instead of assuming that their partner should know what they need, each person accepts the responsibility that it is up to them to share what they feel, and what they want or need from the other. This stage is more healthy and stable than the

290

honeymoon stage, because the individuals bring more experience, wisdom and maturity to the relationship.

Is the Great Psychologist interested in communication? It is John who began his gospel narrative describing Him as the Word, existing before time with His Father. The Greek word here is "logos," meaning "word" or "reason." [108]John continues by stating that the Word became flesh—and dwelled among us. We call Him Jesus. He was and is the expression of God. He is God's movement to communicate with us.

This is the eternal Word, the word of hope, of love, of compassion, of our future. This Word became embodied as a human being. Jesus, the Great Communicator. He came not only to battle the forces of evil, and to give His life for us, but to dialogue with God's creation, you and me!

Some people declare they don't hear God. I believe them. However, if all through your life you have diminished the voice of God to a faint whisper, what do you expect? Let me assure you that the message is being sent, and if we don't hear it, it is we who are the problem. God has been communicating with you at every turn in your life since your birth. The key questions here are "Are you listening?" "Is your antenna up?" I believe without question that the Great Psychologist was a good communicator. His words quickly went straight to the listeners' hearts.

He not only spoke well, he was also a good listener. He still listens! If you sat down across from Him today, He would say, "I hear and know what you are saying!" Within your heart you would know this to be true. When Jesus promises that He will be with us, He is saying that He is listening to you. If you are listened to by the Great

Psychologist of life, this is His gift from Him to you. What you are receiving is a wonderful gift to give to your children, to those around you whom you love, to those who work along side of us, and to those who desperately seek a listening ear.

The heart of communication is not simply a sharing of ideas, thoughts and feelings, but a sharing of oneself. The flow of energy and ideas to be effective is to flow from us as well as to us. From communication there can come a deep understanding of the other person. This feeling of understanding usually leads one to feel close or connected to the other person. This is a love-bond, as I am going to term it, and can exist between friends, children and parents, as well as couples.

The dividend that comes from this deep understanding is the wonderful gift of intimacy. Tragically this is what so many relationships lack. Countless individuals flood the offices of therapists and complain that intimacy is lacking in so many of their relationships. Yet so many do not know how to attain that which they seek because they have not been given the gift themselves. Intimacy builds upon this understanding to produce a deep sense of caring that reaches out to the other person. This significant ingredient helps us to feel connected to the other person. None of this occurs without vulnerability, where the floodgates of our hearts are open to receive and to give.

Communication has the greatest potential of knocking down barriers that separate us from God. It has the greatest potential to knock down the walls that separate us from others.

Questions to Ponder:

1. How would you rate yourself as a communicator?
2. Do you know how to listen?
3. How many people in your life do you think you really know and understand?

Psychological Insight

God has send Jesus to be His Word, and to be the great communicator. Communication is essential to every relationship in life. The better you do it, the better the quality of the relationship. The gift of communication is to understand the other person and to give yourself as well. The dividends of communication are the ingredients of feeling connected and feeling intimate. Communication is hard work, work at it every day. Learning to listen takes time, and it is a skill that can be developed.

"If you have never been frightened by the teachings of Jesus, perhaps you haven't understood them."

He Said to Stop Chasing What You Can't Keep

"I am not trying to take it with me, just trying to stretch it out until I go!"

At least sixty-two tombs of the early Pharoahs are found in the Valley of Kings, on the west bank of the Nile across from Thebes, an isolated place in Egypt. Not far away in Giza are the pyramids, built by thousands of workmen and artisans, and the burial sites of the rich and famous Pharaohs. An Egyptian Proverb says, "Everyone fears time, but time fears the pyramids."

The Egyptians had a unique belief that after death they had to pass through the dangers of the underworld to attain an afterlife of bliss in the Field of Reeds. Anyone who lived a righteous life was eligible, but the catch was that the quality of that future life would depend on the provisions available here. Consequently, the rich had a better chance of bliss in the afterlife. Believing this to be true, they buried alongside of them jewelry, beds, tables, chairs, chariots, and boats. They even buried their pets. They made every effort within their power to take what they had in this world and to carry it with them into the afterlife.

Since the physical body was also to be reunited after death, it was important to preserve the body for the quality of life after death as well. They used their knowledge to embalm the body with its organs, and they have left behind an unusual number of mummies.

Today the ninety pyramids, the temple, majestic monuments and beautiful statues are still standing on this side of eternity for the entire world to see and enjoy. The efforts of the Pharaohs to take the belongings with them has clearly failed. So much of their life was a preparation for death, and the life beyond. Yet, in the end it has all been left behind, on displays in museums for us to enjoy.

Over the years, I have presided over about one hundred funerals. Of all the funerals I have performed, I noticed that there was never a U-Haul with the person's belongings following the casket to the cemetery. As much as you try, you just can't take it with you! However, there are attempts made. Perhaps you read about the man in California who died with an unusual request: He wanted to be buried in his gold-plated Cadillac. As one of the workers at the graveside was shoving the dirt on the Cadillac, he made a "Freudian slip" and said, "Man, that is living!"

Unfortunately, money has become a celebrity in our present society, and everyone seems to be chasing it. Money has become a god to be worshiped. Someone once informed me money could not buy three things: your health, personal happiness, or a baby's smile. It's true!

I still remember a visit I had to a delightful family who lived in Detroit. Their house was situated in Grosse Pointe, beautiful and magnificent enough to accommodate the CEO of any company. Coffee cup in hand, I followed Dorothy as she led me into a huge living room. Dorothy and her husband Ed owned their own printing company, which was very successful. Both of them exhibited a wonderful spirit of faith and commitment and were a wonderful part of the church I was serving.

As she talked about Ed, she described the pain that he constantly lives with. Ed walks with a slight limp, and is hunched over because of a deformity from birth. One can tell it is an effort. In recent years his arthritis has been extreme and he appears to be in constant anguish and discomfort. However, on any given Sunday one would never guess this to be true. Ed is usually at the back of the church with dozens of children gathered around him. Sometimes you will see the children go up and put their hands into his suit pocket. This is okay with Ed, because he knows what they are searching for— a piece of candy. When I left their home that day, I was struck by the irony of the situation. Here was a family that could purchase probably anything they desired. They lived in a home many would envy, and yet their money could not buy one day of health for Ed.

This chapter is about what will last in life and what won't. God has never said to us, "Meet me at the rapture— and bring with you your checkbook, mutual funds, and stocks." Instead, He simply says "Just show up." In fact, this is a "come as you are" event.

Often, the more we have in life the greater the temptation to believe we do not need to rely on the Great Psychologist. Jesus wasn't against wealth and riches, He was against the preoccupation of chasing material things and money. That which occupies our time and energy will sooner or later become our God. Consequently, the saying is true, "where your treasure is, there your heart will be also." What is your heart?

We continue to say money can't buy us happiness, but we keep trying anyway. Perhaps it is because deep within our hearts we know it is "the right thing" to say, but we don't really believe it.

Recently, Fox TV aired an unusual special, "Who Wants to Marry a Multi-millionaire?" Over 23 million viewers tuned in. I view it as the visible, tragic sign of the dysfunction of our present society. Someone called it legal prostitution and they may be correct. In the last segment of the show, the five remaining contestants women paraded before the would-be groom in beautiful wedding gowns. More than one of the women tried to convince the many viewers that this wasn't about money or riches but the relationship that they would have with the groom. I wonder if fifty women would be contestants for "Who Wants to Marry a Poor Man With a Loving Heart?" or "Who Wants to Marry a Dedicated, Responsible Christian?" Yes, I am sure that would have changed it all! While the contestants appeared sincere and looked like they were psychologically together, I am still puzzled that anyone who would marry a stranger for money. Watch out! Your dysfunction may be showing.

The worst thing is taking what is sacred—marriage—and making it non-sacred. In this setting marriage was nothing but a publicity stunt.

So along comes Jesus, the Great Psychologist who simply says "Stop chasing what you cannot keep!" Don't underestimate Him He means it!

Jesus was not against money and riches. What He warns us against is putting anything before His kingdom. Only God can be first, nothing else.

Perhaps what Jesus was concerned about is best illustrated in this story. A rich man showed up at the home of a Rabbi. The Rabbi was concerned about his preoccupation with his money. Rather than preach to the man, he took him to a window overlooking the town. He said "Look out the window and tell me what you see." The rich man obliged and answered, "People." Then the Rabbi led him to a mirror and asked him to look into it. "What do you see?" The man answered, "Myself." The Rabbi said, "Both the window and mirror are glass, but as soon as we add a little silver to the back side of the glass, all you see is yourself."

Isn't it psychologically unhealthy to put things before our relationships? Why all the fuss to gain the whole world to the exclusion of our souls? Why grasp what won't last and give up what will?

Suppose, however, we ask this question: "What can we use here and there as well?" On one side of our life there is the perishable, and on the other side there is imperishable. The question then is, "What is transitional?" What will be meaningful here as well as there; what can I take with me?"

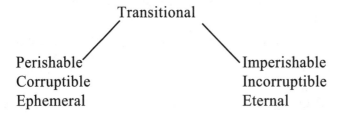

Transitional

Perishable   Imperishable
Corruptible   Incorruptible
Ephemeral   Eternal

Faith will last, as will righteousness, truth, hope and integrity, just to name a few. Meaningful relationships are always a priority; people are the joy of life. The ultimate relationship with God will span all time. Paul tells us our bodies here in this dimension of time are perishable, but they will be raised as imperishable. These things are worth chasing and keeping! All of these I have termed transitional because they span (transition) from one time dimension to the other.

Vicky, a woman in her early forties, sat in my office trying to decide if she should be in my office or a lawyer's! She felt depressed and felt abandoned by her family. Her mother had died two years earlier and she felt as if she had lost a good friend. Her father was still alive but she described him as a passive man who was never there for her. Her mother was a self-made woman who had accumulated a sizable amount of money selling real estate.

After her mother's death, the family lawyer called Vicky and told her that he and her father were handling the estate. Since he was a trusted family friend, she accepted this. Now that her mother had died, she reasoned that she and her father would have a better relationship. Instead, her father appeared to be more distant. Then she was surprised when she discovered that her dad had not only purchased a new expensive car, but was moving from their family home into a huge home in a exclusive neighborhood. All of this happened without her father sharing any information. When she called him to ask him about this, he seemed vague and non-committal.

Vicky felt things just didn't seem right—and she soon found out they weren't. What she discovered not only stunned her, but disillusioned her about human nature. Three hundred thousand dollars that was to come to her was stolen by her father. He invested it in mutual funds, and put it in his name only. After two years, he has continued to refuse to answer any of her questions or to put her name on that investment. She feels betrayed and confused by this turn of events. She continues to come for insights on how to maintain herself, and to nurture herself on her own inward journey. However, as of the writing of this book she has not asked for her day in court. As she explains it to me, "This is not about money, it is about love and a relationship. She still sees her father, every week at church at the same service. He smiles across the crowded sanctuary but soon vanishes. We obviously don't need to ask why!

Does she need a lawyer? Maybe? I know for sure she needs a father.

What would it profit a man if he gained the whole world but lost his daughter?

Questions To Ponder:

1. What gifts in your life are transitional—and what gifts will last?

2. Are things and money too important in your life?

3. How are you giving back as a thank you for what you have?

Psychological Insight

Money and material possessions should never become the main focus of our existence. Everything should be in balance. What we do have, we need to share, remembering it is better to give than it is to hoard. We always need to give back to the universe. Seek the things that are valued in God's kingdom. Keep our priorities clear, it is people that count.

He Taught Us to Loosen Up and Laugh

**"The first time you laugh at yourself,
is the time you have finally reached
a new level of maturity."**

It happened when I was in school—if I told you the year, you would realize I am bathing in formaldehyde to stay young! My "second classroom" when I was a student at Hope College was a coffee shop, a melting pot of friendships and ideas. Many delightful conversations occurred over a cup of coffee.

One day, I found myself sitting across the table from the college chaplain, Dr. David Cook. He had spent many years as a missionary to India, and had many interesting experiences in his life. He was a highly successful person who had many pertinent insights to share. Since I had his undivided attention, I asked him what he thought contributed to a successful life.

Jesus Ph.D.

He smiled, and then his face took on a sober look. His silver-gray hair gave him credibility as he peered over his horn-rimmed glasses at me and my fellow students. I was ready for a powerful insight, a profound thought that I could use in my life.

"Have a sense of humor, Tom!" he said, with a smile on his face.

I was dumbfounded. He saw my surprised expression, and repeated his answer again. I remember thinking, "That's it?" but I held my tongue and listened.

"You have to learn how to laugh, and especially laugh at yourself," Dr. Cook said. "If you take life too seriously, you won't be effective."

I have since discovered Dr. Cook gave me some excellent advice. Laughter has the unique ability to lift us out of the weariness of life, and lighten our load. Laughter and loosening up gives us balance. It is a way of taking care of ourselves.

It is utterly amazing to me that it took 2,000 years since the death of Jesus for us to finally have a portrait of Him laughing. Do we really think that the Jesus, who names an impulsive, wimpy, disciple such as Peter, "the rock," doesn't have a sense of humor?

It's no accident that the first miracle that Jesus did occurred at a wedding, where Jesus was relaxing and people were partying and having fun. Jesus and his family were invited guests. It is in this setting that Jesus made the water into wine, at his mother's urging. He didn't skimp on the quality! The guests recognized it as great wine.

Jesus constantly retreated to the home of Lazarus and his two sisters, Mary and Martha, in order to loosen up, to relax, and enjoy life. He obviously enjoyed their conversation and friendship. As one reads the Scriptures, it appears to be one of His favorite places to be.

Imagine producing a whole generation of those who follow the Great Psychologist and had great fun doing so. For far too long, we have produced generations of intense and far-to-serious disciples who portrayed that the kingdom may not be a joyous place to be. Why not a generation who accepts all of His great truths and yet knows how to laugh, to play, to enjoy life? Why not us? We sing, "This is my Father's World." Why not enjoy it? If there is anyone who should enjoy it, it should be His children. Perhaps they missed the Old Testament verse, [109]"Make a joyful noise to the Lord." These were the words the Israelites used when they began worshiping God.

Frankly, I have learned to be suspicious of those who don't loosen up. Life is serious, and we don't need to make it more serious. I used to be a very serious individual. I know how easily overly-serious people miss out on life! They run the risk of distorting life, even while they think they are holding it sacred. What is life? It is a mist that appears for a little while and is gone. Yet, it is creative, explosive, dynamic, exciting, vital, filled with enthusiasm and spontaneous. If you are bored with life, look to yourself!

If we put it in a formula, it would look like this:

Intensity and seriousness + without loosening up = dullness and duty

Those who don't relax, loosen up, and enjoy life may see life as a misery to be endured, or something to suffer through. In Medieval times, life was seen as a purgatory, and all that people looked forward to was "pie in the sky, by and by"—eternal life.

These are the people who come into my office and sit on the edge of the couch, instead of relaxing. They watch the clock and wonder if they are getting their money's worth. They feel guilty if they are inactive. They often expect too much from other people, and are driven by duty, rather than love. They don't enjoy life, or appreciate the beauty of the moment. They worry about what they should be doing.

The opposite of "loosening up" is being "too tight." When we don't loosen up, we have a tendency to hold on too tight—too tight to our family, too tight to our problems, too tight to life itself.

Carol had read almost every self-help book out there, and her sessions with me were intense. She went to every seminar on recovery she could find, and she even joined a support group. She was serious about her recovery. It is always a delight to have someone come in who is highly-motivated, and Carol soaked up each word I said like a sponge.

A year earlier, she had come in for her first appointment. She was in the middle of divorce, which was very confusing to her. Jeff was unable to support the family financially and did not seem sensitive to her needs. Coming from a rural community in Canada, he seemed to be content to be laid back and to take life as it came. Thus she ended up often supporting both of them, which she resented.

To add to their problems, Jeff was not there in the critical moments of her life, especially during the death of her father. Consequently, they missed several potential growth opportunities in their relationship. For a year, Carol worked through her brokenness. She took the responsibility for her mistakes in the relationship. She actively participated in all of her sessions with questions and a sense of searching. She was surprised to find out how angry she was—at life, at Jeff, and especially at herself.

Carol was exhausted, emotionally raw from her traumatic experiences and hard work in therapy. Then one day she called and said that she was not going to make her appointment. She needed a break from therapy, and wondered if I thought she was ready for graduation. I told her that she still had some work to do, especially in understanding men and picking the right person in her life. This is not an uncommon problem which many women face: When they need a therapist the most to help them make significant decisions in their lives, they are not in therapy. So many are swept away by moments of "love" only to find out that once again they used poor judgment.

However, Carol had analyzed the past in hopes of understanding it, and now she needed to be focused on her present and new decisions. These were pivotal to her future happiness and success. I was not trying to keep her in therapy, and in the end I shared with her that she had gained the basic tools she needed. It was time for her to try her own wings. I was confident that she would be okay.

It was time for Carol to loosen up, to play, and to laugh. It was time for her to thoroughly enjoy life and focus on her successes. She has entered into a new phase of her therapy that only life can teach her. This business of life is serious, but the gift of life is to appreciate its fullness, its joy. This too is life, life that the Great Psychologist wants us to embrace.

The downside to being too intense is that the little things of life and relationships often get magnified into bigger things. That is because we often over-focus on issues. Jim was that way. He analyzed and rationalized everything his wife did. You couldn't say he was wrong, but there was something which also nagged at you to say, "He may not be right, either." Why does everything have to be analyzed, why does it have to be picked apart, why don't we let the little things go? When Jim and his wife both began to relax, to swim with the tide of life, instead of swimming against it, their lives improved.

If ever a man might have lived with good reasons not to loosen up, if ever a man might have lived and looked at life too seriously, if ever a man might have lived too intensely, it would have been Jesus. Suffering and death were imminent in His life. Yet Jesus did not miss the joys of life. He enjoyed each moment, and was enchanted with life. He loosened up, and took care of Himself. He made time for others. He ventured into the depths of life, and celebrated its heights. He measured life by its quality.

A few years ago, several famous people in their twilight years were asked what they would have done differently if they could live life over again. They said they would have played more, taken more time off, breathed the fresh air, saw more sunsets, enjoyed their children more. One said she would have walked barefoot through the flowers!

If we loosen up now, laugh at life, laugh at others, and celebrate life with all of its beauty and mystery, there will be no need for regrets. There will be no need to look back with lingering thoughts. Today would be a good day to begin! Maybe a picnic?

Questions to Ponder:

1. When is the last time you had a good laugh?
2. Do you get accused of taking life too seriously? Are you too intense?
3. Are you playing enough?

Psychological Insight

A sense of humor is critical. Learn to laugh at yourself, and not take yourself too seriously. Don't be critical. Life is exciting! As you see the lighter side of life, it will balance your view of life and help you achieve wholeness.

He Didn't Teach
a Quick Fix

*"One thing at a time, all things in succession.
That which grows slowly endures."*
— *J.G. Hubbard*

She had what we might term as a "female problem."
She was bleeding from her vaginal area and the intensity
of it made her realize that the problem was serious. When
it first happened, she had hoped the problem would go
away, but it did not. When the problem persisted, she
sought the advise of a reputable physician. He stated that
he knew what the problem was, explained it to her, and
told her what he wanted her to do. She followed the
doctor's orders, but she continued to hemorrhage. After
many attempts, she realized that the doctor could not help
her.

She asked around and received names of other doctors
who were considered to be knowledgeable doctors. Some
didn't want to take the case, others said they could help

and didn't, until she finally she became frustrated. Nothing seemed to work. Some remedies helped for a little while, but then she returned to the same fearful problem. Nothing stopped her internal bleeding.

She pursued this path for over ten years, until she was out of money and the personal problem she was facing still there. She was not cured of the problem that plagued her. Desperate, broke, and depressed, she finally gave up. As depressing as it was, this was a problem she would have to learn to live with. So for approximately twelve years that is exactly what she did—accepted it and lived with it. Since she did not have insurance coverage this endeavor cost her all of her savings.

Then one day she received some information that changed her life. Some of her neighbors told her that there was a healer who might be able to help her. He would soon visit the small town where she lived. Perhaps she thought, " I can talk to Him, and get His opinion. Better yet, perhaps he can heal me."

However, the day of his arrival came and there was a huge crowd of people around him. Instead of a moment of privacy, He was totally surrounded by individuals, all trying to get His attention. She was not about to embarrass herself by repeating before a group of people such a personal problem. That is when she came up with her "if only" idea. She thought, "If only I could get close to Him and touch a piece of his clothing, I could be healed of this ugly problem." If it worked, she didn't need to explain anything to anyone.

And that is exactly what she did. She touched a piece of his clothing and within moments, she was healed. A cleansing power surged through her body and she knew that her long-awaited moment of healing had come. She was elated, excited beyond belief. How simple it had been. She began to disappear back into the crowd from which she came, hoping to hurry home. To her, it was a modern miracle!

The Great Healer turned around, looked into the crowd, and said, [110]"Who touched me?" Peter was surprised at Jesus' question since so many people were brushing up against Him. He said, "Master, the crowds surround you and press in on you." But Jesus persisted, [111]"Someone touched me; for I noticed that power had gone from me." When the woman realized that she could not stay hidden in the crowd, she stepped forward and declared she had touched Jesus, and then told Him why she had touched Him.

Jesus said to her, [112]"Daughter, your faith has made you well; go in peace."

Did she believe in a quick fix? Apparently, but let's not be too harsh with her because she's not much different than many of us. Notice what she did in this story: She ran in, touched Him, plugged into the power of Jesus, unplugged from the power, and blended back into the crowd. All this with the hope of being healed, yet remaining anonymous. She didn't said anything, didn't verbally ask for anything, didn't say thank you and suddenly was gone. "Not so," said Jesus. "It is not that easy. No quick fixes."

In other words, if you want the power of healing, you must recognize the Giver of the power.

The woman was confronted by Jesus. She explained why she did what she did, and that she believed He could heal her. No doubt she explained how desperate she had become. Then Jesus made it clear that the power she received was because of her faith, and with that she went away rejoicing.

This woman shows the typical approach many of us take in dealing with God. We use God, plug in when it is convenient, take what we want and then try to disappear back into the crowd without being confronted by the Highest Power of the universe. Other times we pull God off the mantel in our homes, talk about Him on a Sunday, and then place Him back on the mantel for another week. We never allow Him to enter the rest of our daily lives. Such faith is cheap and definitely fragile.

Joe smiled at me when he said it, but I felt he was probably half-serious. "Tom, come on, give me a quick fix." We both laughed, but after Joe left my office, I thought "How ridiculous, this was only his fourth visit." I stopped laughing and thought about his case. There were years of dysfunctional behavior, years of self-defeating patterns of behavior, years of distorted thinking and now—a quick fix. No, I don't think so, not even jokingly. Interestingly enough, Joe dropped out of therapy two weeks later.

Joe was thirty-seven years-old, and had been a chronic liar all of his life. His lying had already ruined his marriage and cost him a job. His friends tolerated him and knew for years he was not authentic with them. A quick fix? Was he joking? Joe, where are you?

Quick fixes don't last. Someone has compared therapy to peeling an onion. It may take years to peel back the layers that have grown over time, and to finally get at the core. This is a slow progress. And usually when we get to the core we discover a woundedness that still needs the healing touch of new insights.

Quick fixes don't last because they usually don't have enough soil to grow in. They have not taken root. They don't get enough nutrients. The next crisis quickly uproots them out of their shallow ground. A quick fix is not only unrealistic, but it often shows our impatience.

A loving father went with his little daughter, Amy, to purchase some seedlings. Amy was very excited about this adventure and her dad allowed her to put the potted seeds in her room and watch them grow. Her dad explained that the sunshine and her watering them when they were dry would nurture them to become beautiful flowers. Amy couldn't wait. She carefully looked after them, day after day. Dad would look into her room occasionally to check on the progress. Then one week, Dad had to leave for a business trip. When he came back, Amy was awake and eager to see her father. However, when he asked how the seedlings were doing, Amy became silent and a tear ran down her cheek. Dad, sensing something was wrong, took her by the hand, and said, "Let's go look." Amy reluctantly went with him. Dad was surprised by what he saw. All the seedlings were pulled out of the dirt. They were lifeless. "Amy, what happened?" Dad asked.

"Well," replied Amy, "they weren't growing fast enough so I pulled them up a little bit every day."

Impatience and unrealistic expectations are at the heart of the quick fix. Both short-circuit the necessary progress of a steady and continuous growth.

The Wonderful Counselor knows the best things in life take time!

Questions to Ponder:

1. What still needs to be fixed or healed in your life?

2. What "quick fixes" have you tried? Did they fail?

3. Are you willing to ask God for His Healing power without manipulating Him?

Psychological Insight

The healing and growth one needs in life takes time, be patient and try the process of healing. Remember, problems that have mounted during many years will take persistent hard work to change. There are no meaningful quick fixes. Take one day at a time.

In a world that is clearly dysfunctional,
the presence of One who is not
makes the world very uneasy!

Jesus: the Catalyst for Change and Growth

"Without growth, all living things die."

Our investigation of Jesus, Ph.D., has been a careful look at change and growth. His insights and principles cannot do anything but lead us toward health and balance. What is so surprising is that so many are content to vegetate and stagnate. The invitation of the Great Psychologist is the invitation to change your life and attain a quality of life that is unequaled.

The great American poet Henry Wadsworth Longfellow lived to the mature age of seventy-five. He was a productive writer to the very end of his life. When someone asked him the secret of his physical wellness and mental alertness, it is said Longfellow pointed to a nearby tree, and asked, "You see that apple tree? It is very old, but I never saw prettier blossoms than those. The tree grows a little new wood each year, and I suppose it is out of the new wood that those blossoms come. Like the apple tree, I try to grow a little new wood each year."

Jesus Ph.D.

My chiropractic friend, Dr. Tony Morici, continues to tell me that many people believe that when one grows old, they slow down. The opposite is true! When one slows down, they grow old. His statement illustrates how growth or a lack of growth can affect our body as well as our mind. Such principles are the exploration of this book and especially this closing chapter.

When I was twenty-seven years old, I had a life-changing experience. I was serving a little rural church in Michigan, and as was our custom on Christmas Day, several elders would meet with me, talk about the service, and then we would pray together. Despite the joy of the holiday, I was deeply troubled, and told them I was admitting myself into a psychiatric hospital the very next day. Their joyful faces suddenly looked puzzled and concerned.

They wanted to know how long I would be there, and I told them, "When the doctors say I am ready to go home, then I will come home. Until that time, I will be there."

It was extremely humbling for a young man who had just finished seven years of higher education and thought he had all the answers to be admitted to a psychiatric hospital. At times I felt that I was running out into the world saying, "Look! I got a B.A. and an M.A.," and the world was laughing at me and saying, "Sit down and I will teach you the rest of the alphabet."

But all of my unresolved issues from my teenage years and young adulthood had finally accumulated to a lethal point. Publicly I was functioning, but behind the scenes I was a wreck. For fifty days I sat in the hospital and listened in a more receptive way than I ever had in my life. I talked about my relationship with my father, which had been estranged. I laughed, I cried, I was up and then I was definitely down. During that time, doctors and professional staff took me apart piece by piece and saw what was there, and then started putting me back together again. It was one of the most painful experiences of my life. At times I felt completely worthless and broken, and wondered if there was any good in me to pull together.

Some of the most significant changes in my thinking occurred during my stay in the hospital. However, I worried incessantly that I would be branded as a "problem child," and that it would ruin any future work I would do in the church. After I returned to the pastoral work, I felt isolated. I sat in my office for a month with my phone sitting silently on my desk. Then one Monday morning the phone rang. It never stopped ringing. People told me that a person honest enough to face his own problems could perhaps help them as well! People came out of the woodwork to ask for help. Suddenly, I felt more effective and I knew I had something to share with them. I still feel that way today.

The changes and growth we experience, no matter how painful, only make us more valuable in God's kingdom. Being fully human and fully vulnerable makes it more possible for the Great Psychologist to use us.

Older clients used to throw out the cliché, "You can't teach an old dog new tricks." However, no one who knows me ever says that in my office! Perhaps they realize there would be zero tolerance for such a statement.

What is it that makes one person open and another closed to growth and change? It may depend on the barriers we build around ourselves. Some of us form a shell around ourselves that lets no information in, some of us let a little information in, and some of us actually allow too much information in and no longer know what we believe.

The key here is balance. We need to have the ability to accept new ideas, and still be grounded and know what we believe. Flexibility will also be a key to our success. Flexibility means we may change the method of our message, but not the message itself. This means we can change, grow and continue to keep our equilibrium. If we charted these thoughts, they would look like this:

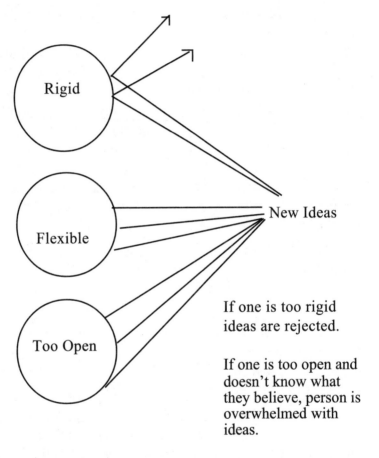

If one is too rigid ideas are rejected.

If one is too open and doesn't know what they believe, person is overwhelmed with ideas.

A phenomenon in our society is that we have changed our concept of the learning curve, but also our concept of the aging process. In the 1950s, when someone retired, they didn't work again and felt useless. They waited around to die. With that attitude, many didn't have to wait too long!

Look how far we have come. Today, people are retiring earlier with the idea of going back to school, and beginning new careers. We are producing a generation of late-bloomers! We've changed our concept about what is old, and what our capacity is to learn. Couple this with a life expectancy that is pushing 80, and it is clear we have a whole new world, and certainly a healthy one! We are living in exciting times.

Our capacity to change and grow has not changed, the only thing that has changed is our thinking about it.

Several things are helpful to think about:

- Always listen with an earnest effort to understand
- Be willing to get out of your comfort zone
- Accept truth wherever you find it
- Remember that pain may be your friend
- Your lowest moment may turn out to be your highest moment

Benjamin Franklin wrote his own epitaph before his death, which was:

Revised Edition

The Body Of Benjamin Franklin, Printer (Like the cover of an old book, Its contents torn out, And stripped of its lettering and gilding.) Lies here food for worms. Yet the work itself shall not be lost, For it will (as he believes) appear once more In a new And beautiful Edition Corrected and Amended By The Author

You will not always be like Jesus, your catalyst for change. Sometimes the Great Psychologist pulls, and other times He pushes. Sometimes He lifts up, and other times He smashes down. Sometimes he helps your brokenness to happen. Seldom does He let you rest on your laurels. During His time on earth, He was often outspoken, blunt, and to the point.

Jesus said we cannot put new wine into old wineskins successfully.[113] When this happens, the new wine ferments, and will burst the old skins. In the same way, Jesus said we cannot put a new patch of cloth on an old garment. Jesus is sharing with us an analogy about new ideas and old paradigms. Many of His contemporaries were trying to take His new ideas and fit them into their old system. No wonder much of what He said didn't make sense to them! Jesus was really saying, "Why not simply have a new model, one not tied to preconceived ideas and structure." His truths, His kingdom, were all part of the new paradigm, just as we are a part of His new creation.

Laziness is a threat to our growth. I have discovered that if I do not drive myself, I have a tendency to hang back, to procrastinate, to become lazy and not get things done. I fully realize that I am always going to be my greatest enemy. Laziness rules many of our lives. We claim that the Word of God is life and truth, and then we seldom read it. We claim certain things are helpful to our growth and others a deterrent to it, yet we seldom do what we need to do to nurture ourselves. We blame things on our busy schedules and too little time, but in the end it is simply our laziness that is at fault. Perhaps the truth is that we have not ventured far beyond the Garden of Eden experience with what ails us.

Every time you break out of your comfort zone, see the experience as a positive one. It may take courage to stay there, but assure yourself that you will grow! Don't let anxiety put you back where you started. If you continue to break out of your comfort zone, these challenges will be fertile ground for change and growth. You won't be disappointed!

When I think of comfort zones, I think of Marie. After working as an administrative assistant, she was promoted to office manager. It was a difficult transition for Marie. For a year she was out of her comfort zone. The people around her questioned her authority, and the power structure that should of supported her failed. Marie believed in herself, and had strong family support, so she persevered. God and Marie had many prayerful conversations during this time! Her dividend is that while the time working has been uncomfortable, she has grown tremendously. You can never stay in your comfort zone and grow.

Jesus is the Great Psychologist. He has the purest insights into your life. He gives us unconditional love and respect. When Jesus asks you to change, He expects you to respond with your best, whole-hearted effort. Remember, He will never ask you to do what you cannot do.

However, Jesus does not ask you to change for the sake of change alone. He asks you to change and move upward toward God and His kingdom. It is a change that spirals up toward the Great Psychologist, who adds a mysterious, supernatural dimension to life that no one else can. He adds the ingredient of His Spirit. This is truly the Spirit of Change.

This is not a gimmick, an inanimate object or thing, but a vital, living, force Who has all of the power of the Godhead to effect what Jesus intends for you. This is the same Spirit who prays for us when our expressions are only groans without words. This is more than empowerment—this is creative explosion!

This concept is not a neat therapeutic tool to make you feel good, but rather a dynamic reality. It is a phenomenon that is not of this world. If we put this concept into a formula, it would look like this:

Your energy + God's energy = lasting change
+ a dividend = Everlasting blessing
Or Your power + God's power = lasting change
+ everlasting communion with Him

For the changes we make, He offers us an unchanging eternal gift.

When I went to Italy, I had a chance to view Michelangelo's magnificent statue of David in Florence. It is one of the greatest sculptures in history! The Carrara marble block that Michelangelo used sat rejected in a work yard for thirty-five years. Yet Michelangelo used it to sculpt his towering David. One man's reject turned into another man's treasure. The statue of David is the epitome of victory over the threatening giants in life. It stands seventeen-feet tall, bulging with youthful energy. David has a keen and confident look in his eyes.

What others have rejected can be turned by a skillful artist into a priceless masterpiece.

Over 2,000 years ago, a man walked a dusty road and saw people who suffered from such horrible diseases that they were isolated from the general population. Others he saw were considered politically incorrect and snubbed. Still others were considered traitors because they were agents of the government and collected taxes. Some were sinful and outcasts. Others were born on the wrong side of the tracks.

This man was called a teacher, a spiritual leader, a prophet, the Son of God. He was and is all of these things and more! Because he fully understands the human mind and the human heart He is the Great Psychologist. He accepts what others reject, and makes them into majestic and magnificent works of art. He molds and shapes them into what is beautiful in the eyes of His Father. You and I are a result of His efforts.

The Great Psychologist offers change and growth, if only you believe! And the greatest change of all has been promised to us. It lies in the not-so-distant future. The exact time has not been revealed to angels or even to Him. Only His Father knows! When that appointed time comes, as He rules from the throne of life, He will declare, [114]"Behold, I make all things new." He promises the ultimate change as we enter a new, complete, and fulfilling life with Him.

Do not be afraid to entrust your life—present and future—to the One who knows what is best for you.

Remember, He is the Author of change.

He is God's chosen Son.

He is the Alpha and Omega of Life.

He is the Great Psychologist!

JESUS 12 STEP PROGRAM

1. *Accept the belief that the Highest Power in the Universe Is God, Our Father.*

2. *We are helpless to save ourselves from our human predicament without help from God.*

3. *Pray to God on a daily basis and remain in constant contact.*

4   *Don't judge others, and if you must judge, judge yourself and take responsibility for your words and actions*

5. *Keep the Kingdom of God as your priority and what you need will be given to you.*

6. *Love people, and treat everyone, regardless of race, creed or status as a child of God.*

7. *Live by your faith and believe all things are possible. They are!*

8. *Forgive on a daily basis and remember that is how you are forgiven.*

9. *Use your personal gifts wisely and in all things glorify God.*

10. *Take control of every aspect of life.*

11. *Worry is meaningless and unproductive. Believe that in every moment of your life God is present and will care for you.*

12. *Seek truth and wisdom in every word and deed in your life, for it leads to eternal life.*

Thomas A. Bruno

POSITIVE STEPS TOWARD
BREAKING CODEPENDENCY

1.   *Be authentic in all your relationships. Be yourself. If you can't be real in the relationship you are in, you arein the wrong relationship.*

2.   *Learn how to say "No" and mean it. If there is something you don't want to do, say so and stick to it.*

3.   *Express your true feelings without stuffing them. You have a right to your feelings.*

4.   *Take care of yourself, no one will do this for you. Do things that make you happy and make you feel good about yourself and life.*

5.   *Control no one but your own life. Control your finances, your emotions and your behavior, everything else is off limits.*

6.   *Focus on your life and the challenges you face. Solve your own problems and let others solve theirs.*

7.   *Understand your boundaries and don't let others cross them. Be respectful of the boundaries others have set.*

8.   *Remember you are worthy of the gifts that come into your life. Receive them gracefully without rejection and say "thank you."*

9.   *Don't manipulate others through guilt, and don't allow yourself to be.*

Between us and heaven or hell there is
           only   life,
which   is   the   frailest   thing
           in   the   world.
—Blaise   Pascal   Pensee's   (1670)

Footnotes

1. *T.S. Eliot, The Complete Poems and Plays, 1909-1950.* Harcourt, Inc. New York, 1962. p.56
2. Luke 17:21
3. Psalm 42:5
4. Luke 9:53
5. Mark 8:32
6. Matthew 14:28-30
7. Matthew 14:30
8. Matthew 17:20
9. Matthew 15:28
10. Luke 8:44
11. John 11:38-40
12. Matthew 9:28-29
13. Mark 11:23
14. Matthew 9:28
15. Luke 4:43
16. John 12:27
17. Luke 2:49
18. Mark 10:15
19. Luke 22:42
20. Luke 22:44-45
21. Matthew 26:42
22. Matthew 16:13-20
23. John 1:51
24. Matthew7:7
25. Matthew7:8   & Luke 7:11-17
26. Matthew 6:25-34

27. Matthew 6:25
28. Luke 6:38
29. John 2:47
30. John 1:49
31. Matthew 5:8
32. Philippians 4:8-9
33. I Corinthians 13 entire chapter
34. Matthew 27:40
35. Matthew 27:42
36. Matthew 27:46
37. Luke 23:34
38. Luke 23:43
39. John 19:28
40. John 19:26-27
41. Luke 23:46
42. John 19:29
43. Genesis 3:12-14
44. Genesis 4:9
45. Luke 19:1-10 Story of Zaccheaus
46. John 8:3-11
47. Mark 5:30
48. Luke 15:21
49. Luke 23:39-43
50. Luke 23:43
51. Matthew 23:15
52. Luke 16:15
53. John 7:06
54. John 10:10
55. John 3:8
56. Matthew 4:1-11 Temptation of Jesus in Wilderness
57. Matthew 21:12
58. Matthew 5:22-23
59. John 10:18